ROY HARRIS
AND
INTEGRATIONAL SEMIOLOGY
1956-2015

A BIBLIOGRAPHY

Prepared by David Bade
with the assistance of
Rita Harris and Charlotte Conrad

The International Association for the Integrational Study of
Language and Communication

©2015

The International Association for the Integrational Study of Language and Communication

The IAISLC was founded in 1998. It is managed by an international Executive Committee, whose members in 2014 were:

David Bade (University of Chicago, retired)
Stephen J. Cowley (University of Southern Denmark)
Daniel R. Davis (University of Michigan)
Dorthe Duncker (University of Copenhagen)
†Roy Harris (University of Oxford, Emeritus)
Jesper Hermann (University of Copenhagen)
Christopher Hutton (University of Hong Kong)
Peter Jones (Sheffield Hallam University)
Adrian Pablé (University of Hong Kong)
Nigel Love (University of Cape Town)
Talbot J. Taylor (College of William & Mary)
Michael Toolan (University of Birmingham)
Charlotte Conrad (Dubai)
Jon Orman (Brighton)
Sinfree Makoni (Penn State University)
Rukmini Bhaya Nair (Indian Institute of Technology)

Anyone wishing to join the Association can do so by email apable@hku.hk or by sending their name and address to the Secretary:

Dr Adrian Pablé
School of English
Run Run Shaw Tower
Centennial Campus
The University of Hong Kong
Hong Kong S.A.R

Contents

Preface	v
Introduction	vii
I. Works by Roy Harris	1
II. Reviews of Books by Roy Harris	37
III. Integrational Linguistics and Related Works	
A. Bibliography	53
B. Collections	53
C. Philosophy. Methodology. Semiology	54
D. Descriptive linguistics	69
E. Cognitive linguistics. Biology. Evolution	70
F. History. Historical Linguistics. History of Linguistics	75
G. Writing. Literacy	81
H. Education. Language learning and teaching	88
I. Translation	91
J. Literature	92
K. Arts	94
L. Psychology. Communication	95
M. Anthropology. Ethnology	100
N. Sociolinguistics. Politics. Economics	101
O. Religion	108
P. Law	109
Q. Science. Mathematics	112
R. Communication technologies. Communication at work. Human-computer interaction. Information science	113
Name index	121

Preface

The list of works by Roy Harris from 1956 through 1995 has been taken from "Roy Harris: Publications 1956-1995" published in *Linguistics Inside Out*. The list of publications from 1996 through 2010 was supplied by Rita Harris and slightly altered and updated by David Bade. The altered list of publications from 1996 through 2010 along with a list of book reviews compiled by David Bade were both published in the July 2011 issue (volume 33 nr. 4) of *Language Sciences*. Integrationist related publications have been collected in the Integrationist Repository (www.integrationistrepository.com) by Charlotte Conrad. Material from these four main sources have been edited and supplemented by David Bade who bears sole responsibility for any and all errors and infelicities that discriminating readers may find herein.

David Bade
9 September 2014

Postscript

Roy Harris died on February 9, 2015, as this bibliography was in the course of final editing. I know of two obituaries that will soon be published: John Joseph's "Roy Harris" in *Cahiers Ferdinand de Saussure* and Nigel Love's "Roy Harris (1931–2015)" in volume 43 (2015) of *Language & Communication*. May he rest in peace while his writings continue to disturb the academic mind.

INTRODUCTION

When I embarked upon the project of finding and obtaining reviews of books by Roy Harris a few years ago for the festschrift *Linguistics Out of Bounds: Explorations in Integrational Linguistics*, I did not realize how much I would learn about book reviewing and the reading abilities of professional academics. And having spent many years searching for books and articles on Mongolia in Czech, Hungarian, Polish, Romanian and Slovak, I did not realize how difficult it is to locate specific individuals and their publications in Google when those people write in English on linguistics and have rather common names like Roy Harris. If you have a name and title of a particular book or paper, it is easy to find hundreds of sites like GoogleBooks which will inform you that the author of *The Language Machine* was Robert Harris, born in 1957 in Nottingham (as it did when I checked on 31 August 2011), the University of Sheffield website which notes that Roy Harris had a great influence over the development of the ideas of his student Noam Chomsky (https://sites.google.com/a/sheffield.ac.uk/all-about-linguistics/branches/syntax/who-does-syntax accessed 31 July 2014), or Debrett's peerage which has the note under Publications: N/A. On the other hand, Google and GoogleBooks do allow the searcher to find citations to the work of Roy Harris and other's engaged in integrational linguistics in publications of all sorts, whether the authors of those websites actually engage Harris or integrational linguistics in any way. Yet as any academic researcher knows, far too many papers are packed with references that had no influence at all on the ideas expressed or examined. That is where the real difficulties begin in attempting to study the influence of an author in a more profound manner than counting citations. Those difficulties are both the justification for and the obstacles to overcome in compiling a bibliography such as this one, for its intended scope goes well beyond a list of the writings of Roy Harris and his students.

The works included in this bibliography, while providing an up-to-date list of the publications of Roy Harris do not constitute a canonical list of integrationist writings, nor is such a list possible, let alone desirable. The list is neither definitive nor closed. Precisely because Harris refused to enclose his thought within the boundaries (whose boundaries?) of a particular discipline, his work has been discovered, engaged and developed by a diverse group of scholars who are united only by having a common inspiration in the writings of Roy Harris.

The information scientist Julian Warner was exploring the implications of integrational semiology in his field already in the late 1980s. In his 1997 review of Harris's *The Origin of Writing* (1986) and *Signs of Writing* (1995), Warner wrote "the difficulty of the works and the complexity of the issues addressed is matched by their significance" ("Studying writing"). In France studies of internet use and writing have been greatly influenced by Harris's *La sémiologie de l'écriture* as the authors of *Lire, écrire, récrire* (Jean Davallon, Marie Després-Lonnet, Yves Jeanneret, Joëlle Le Marec and Emmanuël Souchier) acknowledged in their introduction: "Notre recherche se nourrit avant tout de la sémiotique héritée d'Anne-Marie Christin, qui convoque l'idée d'une forme visible donnant accès à une lecture – la « pensée de l'écran », « l'image écrite » –; dans certains de ses développements, elle met à profit l'approche fonctionnelle de Roy Harris qui définit l'écriture comme une intégration du texte dans un contexte". Jerome Bruner wrote recently "You can see, then, why I'm so taken with Roy Harris's bold principle of 'cotemporality'" (in his paper "Narrative distancing: a foundation of literacy") and Kjeld Schmidt acknowledged that "in our attempt to disentangle the web of interlaced semiological practices as (elements of) coordinative practices and to do so meticulously and accountably, the work of the British 'integrational linguist' Roy Harris has proved to be immensely valuable" (in his *Cooperative Work and Coordinative Practices*, p.22-23). In an essay "How do we know what we think we know? Methodological reflections on Jesus research" religious historian and Professor of New Testament studies Stanley E. Porter found in Harris's *The Linguistics of History* "the fundamental linguistic support for successful historical writing" to be applied in historical Jesus research (p. 90).

In my own case I came to appreciate Harris in two very different endeavors. The first was in my attempts to understand the practices and problems of communication in libraries, in particular the work of cataloging in its policy and technical dimensions. Harris's writings brought clarity everywhere, while no other linguistic theory that I had ever studied had proven to be of any value at all in understanding those problems. The second area in which Harris was immensely valuable for me was in grappling with the particular problems of writing a history of the Mongolian invasion of Jawa: not only did his *The Linguistics of History* reorient my approach to the topic, but his general approach to semiology, communication, writing and translation in particular led me to ask questions that bore fruit in a second edition of my own book (*Of Palm Wine, Women and War*).

Yet not all those who have been influenced by Harris acknowledge their debt, and some who have acknowledged an intellectual debt in some publications have continued to develop their ideas in print without further acknowledgement. As an example of the former, when I read Jacques Legrand's *Parlons mongol* it struck me as an outstanding example of how the use of Harris's ideas on writing could inform empirical studies of language and practical textbooks, yet Harris is not mentioned therein. I mentioned this to Legrand when I met him a few years later and he laughed, acknowledging that he had been both impressed and influenced by Harris's *La sémiologie de l'écriture* and that he was always somewhat dismayed to be reminded that his best ideas were someone else's. Many authors (like the present writer) who have been influenced by the writings of Roy Harris do not quote him in every publication that bears the clear marks of his influence, and this greatly complicates the task of determining what to include and which publications to leave out of a bibliography devoted to tracing his influence.

The task that I set myself was to bring together not only the works of Harris (Part I) and the works of those who directly responded to his writings in book reviews (Part II), but to locate as wide a range as possible of works that bear the marks of having been oriented, reoriented or disoriented by an encounter with Harris or any other writings by those who have developed his ideas, whether as integrational linguistics or as some redirecting of those ideas in a seemingly distant domain (such as Khubilai Khan's naval campaign to Jawa). Thus I have included not only the majority of publications (among those that I could locate) by those of his students who developed his ideas and together with Harris formed the original International Association for the Integrational Study of Language and Communication (Daniel Davis, Hayley Davis, Chris Hutton, Nigel Love, Talbot J. Taylor, Michael Toolan, George Wolf) as well as some of the works of other students who sooner or later distanced themselves from Harris's work (e.g. Deborah Cameron, Trevor Pateman), but works by as many of those authors like myself who discovered Harris's writings through their own research projects. Such a broad scope makes it impossible to represent the list that follows as being in any way comprehensive, and I have no doubt that were it possible to trace the influence of Harris's ideas through the works of Crowley, Davis, Hutton, Jeanneret, Jones, Legrand, Love, Mühlhäusler, Pablé, Schmidt, Souchier, Taylor, Toolan, Warner and all others whose works I do know of, the list would be greatly expanded. Yet to identify an influence or an engagement with the ideas developed in Harris's writings is not to identify a single trajectory that one might call "Integrationism" for in the writings of Harris himself one may find no small number of critical responses to the writings of scholars who discuss Harris's ideas and, in Harris's own estimation, misunderstand them in some fundamental way.

In sum, the bibliography that follows provides a complete record of the writings of Roy Harris published during his lifetime (which came to a close on the 9th of February 2015), a comprehensive and chronological but almost certainly incomplete record of the initial critical reception of all of Harris's books in the form of book reviews, and an indication of where these ideas have lead other scholars, both in linguistics and in a wide range of areas traditionally considered beyond the limits of "linguistics proper". Indeed, since my own discovery of the writings of Roy Harris one of my keenest interests has been to identify how his ideas have been received as a philosophical approach rather than a matter of linguistics, and Part III below documents what I have discovered so far in my attempts to understand the fecundity of Harris's ideas and critiques of his predecessors, linguists, philosophers and scholars in all areas.

I. Works by Roy Harris

1. 'The White Stag in Chrétien's *Erec et Enide*'. *French Studies* 1956, 10:1, pp.55-61.
2. 'Et Liconaus ot non ses pere'. *Medium Aevum* 1957, 26:1, pp.32-35.
3. 'A terminus a quo for the Roman de Thebes'. *French Studies* 1957, 11:3, pp.201-2013.
4. Review of W. Ziltener, *Chrétien und die Aeneis*. *Medium Aevum* 1958, 27:3, pp.186-189.
5. Review of G. Tilander, *Mélanges d'étymologie cynégétique*. *Modern Language Review* 1960, 55:3, pp.439-440.
6. Review of F.W. Locke, *The Quest for the Holy Grail*. *Medium Aevum* 1961, 30:3, pp.186-188.
7. Review of H. Adolf, *Visio Pacis*. *Medium Aevum* 1961, 30:3, pp.188-189.
8. Review of L. Thorpe (ed.), *Le Roman de Laurin*. *French Studies* 1961, 15:4, pp.360-361.
9. Review of C. Grassi, *Correnti e contrasti di lingua e cultura nelle valli cisalpine di parlata provenzale e franco-provenzale*. *Modern Language Review*, 1962, 57:1, pp.115-116.
10. Review of C.W. Dunn, *The Foundling and the Werewolf*. *Medium Aevum* 1962, 31:1, pp.70-72.
11. Review of R.A. Haadsma and J. Nuchelmans, *Précis de latin vulgaire*. *Modern Language Review* 1964, 59:3, p.473.
12. Review of S. Heinimann, *Das Abstraktum in der französischen Literatursprache des Mittelalters*. *Medium Aevum* 1965, 34:1, p.83.

13. Review of K. Urwin (ed.), *A Short Old French Dictionary for Students*. ***Medium Aevum*** 1965, 34, pp.83-84.
14. 'Criteria in descriptive semantics'. ***Theoria*** 1966, 32:3, pp.237-239.
15. Review of J.A. Fodor and J.J. Katz (eds.), *The Structure of Language*. ***Mind*** 1966, 75:299, pp. 450-451.
16. "Gallo-Romance third declension plurals". ***Revue de linguistique romane*** 1966, 30:117-118, pp.58-70.
17. "Chansons de geste". *Chambers's Encyclopedia*, New Revised Edition, Oxford, 1966, 3, pp.270-271.
18. "Chrétien de Troyes". *Chambers's Encyclopedia*, New Revised Edition, Oxford, 1966, 3, p.525.
19. "Roman courtois". *Chambers's Encyclopedia*, New Revised Edition, Oxford, 1966, 11, p.757.
20. "François Villon". *Chambers's Encyclopedia*, New Revised Edition, Oxford, 1966, 3, pp.306-307.
21. Review of S. Cigada, *La leggenda medievale del Cervo Bianco e le origini della 'matière de Bretagne'*. ***French Studies*** 1967, 21:1, pp.50-51.
22. "The semantics of self-description". ***Analysis*** 1967, 27:4, p. 142.
23. Review of D'A. S. Avalle, *Latino 'circum romançum' e 'rustica romana lingua'*. ***Medium Aevum*** 1967, 36:1, pp.52-54.
24. "Piedmontese influence on Valdôtain syntax". ***Revue de linguistique romane*** 1967, 31:121-122, pp.180-189.
25. Review of G. Moignet, *Le pronom personnel français*. ***French Studies*** 1967, 31:2, pp.182-183.
26. Review of A.M. Colby, *The portrait in twelfth-century French literature*. ***Medium Aevum*** 1967, 36:2, pp.183-185.
27. Review of R. de Dardel, *Recherches sur le genre roman des substantifs de la troisième declinaison*. ***Modern Language Review*** 1968, 63:1, pp. 239-240.

28. "La structure des paradigmes en latin vulgaire". *Actas del XI Congreso Internacional de Lingüística y Filología Romanicas*, Madrid, 1968, 1, pp. 391-398.
29. Review of L.C. Porter (ed.), Jaques Peletier du Mans, *Dialogue de l'Ortografe e Prononciacion Françoese*. **French Studies** 1968, 22:2, pp.146-147.
30. Review of P. Porteau, *Deux études de sémantique française*. **Modern Language Review** 1968, 63:3, pp.699-700.
31. "Translation propositions". **Linguistica Antwerpiensia** 1968, 2, pp.217-227.
32. Review of R. Posner, *The Romance Languages*. **Modern Language Review** 1968, 63:3, pp.698-699.
33. "Notes on a problem of franco-provençal morphology". ***Zeitschrift für romanische Philologie*** 1968, 84:5-6, pp.572-581.
34. Review of W. Meyer-Lübke, *Historische Grammatik der französischen Sprache. Zweiter Teil: Wortbildungslehre*. **French Studies** 1968, 22:3, pp.266-267.
35. "Self-description and the theory of types" **Analysis** 1968, 28:6, pp.207-208.
36. "Pronominal postposition in Valdôtain". ***Revue de linguistique romane*** 1969, 33:129-130, pp.133-143.
37. "Type-meanings and token-meanings" **Journal of linguistics** 1969, 5:1, pp.143-144.
38. Review of H. Rheinfelder, *Altfranzösische Grammatik, Zweiter Teil: Formenlehre*. **French Studies** 1969, 23:3, p.273.
39. "Semantics and translation". *Actes du Xe Congrès International des Linguistes*. Edited by A Graur. Bucharest: Editions de l'Académie de la République Socialiste de Roumanie, 1970, 2, pp.461-467. Reprinted in Nigel Love (ed.), *The Foundations of Linguistic Theory. Selected Writings of Roy Harris*. London: Routledge, 1990. pp.60-65.

40. "Deviance and citation". *Journal of Linguistics* 1970, 6:2, pp.253-256.
41. "The Strasburg Oaths: a problem of orthographic interpretation". *Revue de linguistique romane* 1970, 34:135-136, pp.403-406.
42. Review of V. Väänänen, *Introduzione al latino volgare*. *Medium Aevum* 1972, 41:1, pp.81-82.
43. "Translation into Martian". *Mind*, 1972, 81:322, p.276.
44. Review of K. Baldinger (ed.), *Dictionnaire étymologique de l'ancien français. Fascicule G1*. *Medium Aevum* 1972, 41:3, pp.294-295.
45. "Performative paradigms". **Transactions of the Philological Society** 1972, 70, pp.44-58. Reprinted in Nigel Love (ed.), *The Foundations of Linguistic Theory. Selected Writings of Roy Harris*. London: Routledge, 1990. pp.66-78.
46. "Words and word criteria in French". F.J. Barnett et al. (eds.), *History and Structure of French: Essays in Honour of Professor T.B.W. Reid*. Oxford: Blackwell, 172. pp.117-133. Reprinted in Nigel Love (ed.), *The Foundations of Linguistic Theory. Selected Writings of Roy Harris*. London: Routledge, 1990. pp.44-59.
47. Review of W.L. Chafe, *Meaning and the Structure of Language*. **Journal of Linguistics** 1973, 9:1, pp.115-120.
48. *Synonymy and Linguistics Analysis*. Oxford: Blackwell, 1973. In the United States and Canada: Toronto and Buffalo: University of Toronto Press, 1973. (Language and Style Series, XII) 166 pp.
49. Review of D.D.R. Owen (ed.), *Arthurian Romance*. **French Studies** 1974, 28:1, pp.52-53.
50. (with Nigel Love) "A note on French nasal vowels". **Linguistics** 1974, 126, pp.63-68.

51. Review of G. Lavis, *L'expression de l'affectivité dans la poésie lyrique française du moyen âge*. **Medium Aevum** 1976, 45:1, pp.114-117.
52. "Early generative semantics". *Journal of Literary Semantics* 1976, 5:2, pp.78-90.
53. "Semantics, performatives and truth". **Journal of Literary Semantics** 1977, 6:2, pp.63-75. Reprinted in Nigel Love (ed.), *The Foundations of Linguistic Theory. Selected Writings of Roy Harris*. London: Routledge, 1990. pp.79-95.
54. *On the Possibility of Linguistic Change*. Oxford: Clarendon Press, 1977. 23 pp.
55. *Communication and Language*. Oxford: Clarendon Press, 1978. 21 pp. Reprinted in Nigel Love (ed.), *The Foundations of Linguistic Theory. Selected Writings of Roy Harris*. London: Routledge, 1990. pp. 136-150.
56. Review of B. Comrie, *Aspect*. **Journal of Literary Semantics** 1978, 7:2, pp.114-117.
57. "Word wars: on thought and language". **Encounter** 1978, 50:3, pp.42-49.
58. "The descriptive interpretation of performative utterances". **Journal of Linguistics** 1978, 14:2, pp.309-310.
59. Review of G.A. Miller and P.N. Johnson-Laird, *Language and Perception*. **Journal of Linguistics** 1978, 14:2, pp.342-347.
60. Review of G. Cannon, *An Integrated Transformational Grammar of the English Language*. **Review of English Studies** 1979, 30:119, pp.324-325.
61. Review of P. Trudgill (ed.), *Sociolinguistic Patterns in British English*. **Review of English Studies** 1979, 30:120, pp.447-449.
62. *The Language-Makers*. London: Duckworth, 1980. US Edition: Ithaca, New York: Cornell University Press, 1980. 194 pp.

63. "The Englishness of English". Review of S. Greenbaum, G. Leech & J. Svartvik (eds.), *Studies in English Linguistics for Randolph Quirk*. **London Review of Books** 6 November 1980, pp.21-22.
64. "Communication about communication". **Language & Communication** 1981 1:1, pp.1-2.
65. "The need for glottotherapy". Review of D. Bolinger, *Language - The Loaded Weapon*. **Times Literary Supplement** 30 January 1981, p. 302.
66. "A passion for words". Review of D. Crystal (ed.), *Eric Partridge: In His Own Words*. **Times Literary Supplement** 30 January 1981, p. 301.
67. "Archisemiotics". Review of G. Broadbent, R. Bunt and C. Jencks (eds.), *Signs, Symbols and Architecture*. **Design Studies** April 1981, pp. 122-123.
68. "The dialect of Fleet Street". Review of K. Waterhouse, *Daily Mirror Style*. **Times Literary Suplement** 22 May 1981, pp.559-560.
69. *The Language Myth*. London: Duckworth, 1981. US Edition: New York: St Martin's Press, 1981. 212 pp.
70. "Scoring the language game". Review of J. Lyons, *Language and Linguistics: an Introduction*. **London Review of Books** 15 October 1981, pp.13-14.
71. "Truth-conditional semantics and natural languages". T.E. Hope et al. (eds.), *Language, Meaning and Style. Essays in Memory of Stephen Ullmann*. Leeds: Leeds University Press, 1981. pp.21-37. Reprinted in Nigel Love (ed.), *The Foundations of Linguistic Theory. Selected Writings of Roy Harris*. Edited by Nigel Love. London: Routledge, 1990. pp.96-111.
72. "Performing in words". Review of E. Goffman, *Forms of Talk*. **Times Literary Supplement** 18 December 1981, pp.1455-1456.

73. "Something every speaker has". Review of J.C. Wells, *Accents of English*. **Times Educational Supplement** 14 May 1982, p.26.
74. "The exchange of signs". Review of R.E. Innis, *Karl Bühler: Semiotic Foundations of Language Theory*. **Times Literary Supplement** 18 June 1982, p. 669.
75. "From Adam to Aarsleff". Review of H. Aarsleff, *From Locke to Saussure*. **London Review of Books** 19 August 1982, pp. 11-12.
76. "The history men". Review of R.W. Burchfield (ed.), *A Supplement to the Oxford English Dictionary: Volume 3*. **Times Literary Supplement** 3 September 1982, pp.935-936.
77. "Means of communication". Review of J.J. Gumperz, *Discourse Strategies*. **Times Literary Supplement** 14 January 1983, p. 37.
78. "Semantics". Review of J. Aitchison, *Language Change: Progress or Decay?* ; R. Chapman, *The Language of English Literature*; R.K. Fenn, *Liturgies and Trials*; J. Lyons, *Language, Meaning and Context*. **Times Educational Supplement** 14 January 1983, p.24.
79. "Beware of standard(s)". **Times Educational Supplement** 25 February 1983, p.2.
80. "Putting the users first". Review of D. Leith, *A Social History of English*. **Times Educational Supplement** 8 April 1983, p.21.
81. "Power and the power of speech". Review of P. Bourdieu, *Ce que parler veut dire*. **Times Literary Supplement** 20 May 1983, p.524.
82. (editor) *Approaches to Language*. Oxford: Pergamon, 1983. (Language & Communication Library, vol. 4)
83. "Language and speech". Roy Harris (ed.), *Approaches to Language*. Oxford: Pergamon, 1983. pp.1-15.

84. Ferdinand de Saussure. *Course in General Linguistics*. Translated by Roy Harris. London: Duckworth, 1983.
85. "Literary translating: theoretical ideas". *Times Literary Supplement* 14 October 1983, p.1119.
86. "The speech-communication model in 20th-century linguistics and its sources". S. Hattori and K. Inoue (eds.), *Proceedings of the XIIIth International Congress of Linguists*. Tokyo, 1983. pp.864-869. Reprinted in Nigel Love (ed.), *The Foundations of Linguistic Theory. Selected Writings of Roy Harris*. London: Routledge, 1990. pp.151-157.
87. "All my eye and Betty Martin". Review of L.G. Pine, *A Dictionary of Mottoes*; J. Green, *Newspeak: a Dictionary of Jargon*; E.S.C. Weiner, *The Oxford Miniguide to English Usage*; A.P. Cowrie, R. Mackin and I.R. McCaig, *The Oxford Dictionary of Current Idiomatic English, vol. II*; K. Hudson, *A Dictionary of the Teenage Revolution and its Aftermath*; E. Partridge, *A Dictionary of Catch-Phrases*. **London Review of Books**, 1 December 1983, pp.12-13.
88. "The misunderstanding of newspeak". *Times Literary Supplement* 6 January 1984, p.17.
89. Review of J. MacNamara, *Names for Things*. **Language Sciences** 1984, 6:1, pp.173-177.
90. "Speaking silently". Review of M. Deuchar, *British Sign Language*. *Times Literary Supplement* 20 July 1984, p.807.
91. "Soft sell and soft soap". Review of D. Crystal, *Who Cares About English Usage?* and W.F. Bolton, *The Language of 1984*. *Times Literary Supplement* 3 August 1984, p.859.
92. "The view from the blackboard". Review of M. Meek and J.Miller (eds.), *Changing English*. *Times Literary Supplement* 14 September 1984, p.2031.
93. "The semiology of textualization". **Language Sciences** 1984, 6:2, pp.271-286. Reprinted in Nigel Love (ed.), *The*

Foundations of Linguistic Theory. Selected Writings of Roy Harris. London: Routledge, 1990. pp.210-226; and in Roy Harris and George Wolf (eds.). *Integrational Linguistics: a First Reader*. Oxford: Pergamon, 1998. pp.227-240.
94. "What was meant by what was said". Review of G.P. Baker and P.M.S. Hacker, *Language, Sense and Nonsense*. **London Review of Books** 20 September 1984, pp.18-19.
95. "Must monkeys mean?". Rom Harré and V. Reynolds (eds.), *The Meaning of Primate signals*. Cambridge: Cambridge University Press, 1984. pp.116-137. Reprinted in Nigel Love (ed.), *The Foundations of Linguistic Theory. Selected Writings of Roy Harris*. London: Routledge, 1990. pp.158-179.
96. "Mizzled". Review of *Longman Dictionary of the English Language*; L. Heller, A. Humez and M. Dror, *The Private Lives of English Words*; B. Bryson, *The Penguin Dictionary of Troublesome Words*; J. Shipley, *The Origins of English Words*; E. Partridge, *A Dictionary of Slang and Unconventional English*, ed. P. Beale. **London Review of Books** 21 February 1958, pp.18-19.
97. (with I. Griffiths) "The semiotics of mental representation". **Semiotica** 1985, 53, pp.179-214.
98. (editor, with Charles-James N. Bailey), *Developmental Mechanisms of Language*. Oxford: Pergamon, 1985. (Language & Communication Library, vol. 6)
99. (with Charles-James N. Bailey) "On developmentalism". Charles-James N. Bailey and Roy Harris (eds.), *Developmental Mechanisms of Language*. Oxford: Pergamon, 1985. pp.vii-xii.
100. "Saussure and the dynamic paradigm". Charles-James N. Bailey and Roy Harris (eds.), *Developmental Mechanisms of Language*. Oxford: Pergamon, 1985. pp.167-183.

101. *The Origin of Writing*. London: Duckworth, 1986. US edition: La Salle, Illinois: Open Court, 1986. ix + 166 pp.
102. "Sherlock Holmes meets the semioticians". Review of Umberto Eco and T.A. Sebeok (eds.), *The Sign of Three*. **Language Sciences** 1986, 8:2, pp.197-201.
103. "No arguing with English". Review of *The Story of English* (BBC 2) and the book by R. McCrum, W. Cran and R. MacNeil. **Times Literary Supplement**, 26 September 1986, pp.1062, 1079.
104. Review of M. Toussaint, *Contre l'arbitraire du signe*. **Language in Society** 1986, 1:3, pp.444-445.
105. "Language difficulties". Review of R. Kirk, *Translation Determined*. **Times Literary Supplement** 28 November 1986, p.1338.
106. "The grammar in your head". C. Blakemore and S. Greenfield (eds.), *Mindwaves*. Oxford: Blackwell, 1987. pp.507-516.
107. *Reading Saussure: A Critical Commentary on the Cours de linguistique générale*. London: Duckworth, 1987. US edition: La Salle, Illinois: Open Court, 1987. xvii + 248 pp.
108. *The Language Machine*. London: Duckworth, 1987. US edition: Ithaca, New York: Cornell University Press, 1987. 182 pp.
109. "The ephemerality of translation". **Times Literary Supplement** 28 August 1987, pp.924, 933.
110. "Mentioning the unmentionable". *International Journal of Moral and Social Studies* 1987, 2:3, pp.175-188.
111. "In and out of the language lab". Review of L.-J. Calvet, *La guerre des langues et les politiques linguistiques* and F.J. Newmeyer, *The Politics of Linguistics*. **Times Literary Supplement** 11 December 1987, p.1373.
112. "Language as social interaction: integrationalism versus segragationalism". **Language Sciences** 1987, 9:2, pp.131-

143. Reprinted in Nigel Love (ed.), *The Foundations of Linguistic Theory. Selected Writings of Roy Harris.* London: Routledge, 1990. pp.197-209; and in Roy Harris and George Wolf (eds.). *Integrational Linguistics: a First Reader.* Oxford: Pergamon, 1998. pp.5-14.
113. "The ideological implications of onomatopoeia in the Eighteenth Century". **Studies in Eighteenth-Century Culture** 1987, 17, pp.209-216.
114. "La traversée du « no man's land »". *Modèles linguistiques* 1987, IX:2, pp.7-10 (French version of "Across the no man's land", no.118 below)
115. "Murray, Moore et le mythe". *Modèles linguistiques* 1987, IX:2, pp.11-38. (French version of "Murray, Moore and the Myth", no.119 below)
116. *Language, Saussure and Wittgenstein: How to Play Games with Words.* London: Routledge, 1988. 136 pp.
117. (editor) *Linguistic Thought in England 1914-1945.* London: Duckworth, 1988.
118. "Across the no man's land". Roy Harris (ed.), *Linguistic Thought in England 1914-1945.* London: Duckworth, 1988. pp.ix-xi.
119. "Murray, Moore and the Myth". Roy Harris (ed.), *Linguistic Thought in England 1914-1945.* London: Duckworth, 1988. pp.1-26.
120. "*Language & Communication*: the first seven years". E.J.J. Maxwell (ed.), *Robert Maxwell and Pergamon Press.* Oxford: Pergamon, 1988. pp.657-659.
121. Review of E.J. Reuland and A.G.B. Ter Meulen (eds.), *The Representation of (In)definiteness.* **History and Philosophy of Logic** 1988, 9:2, pp.250-251.
122. "Who will translate the translators?". *Encounter* 1988, 72:2 pp.68-73.

123. "The semiotic basis of applicative grammar". Review of S. Shaumyan, *A Semiotic Theory of Language*. **Semiotica** 1988, 74:1-2, pp.121-132.
124. "On a sticky wicket". Review of R. Bartsch, *Norms of Language* and S. Greenbaum, *Good English and the Grammarian*. **Times Literary Supplement** 30 September 1988, p.1082.
125. "The worst English in the world?" An inaugural lecture. **Supplement to the Gazette, University of Hong Kong** 24 April 1989, 36:1, pp.37-46.
126. "The Garden of Eden". **Hongkong Standard (Education)** 9 June 1989, p.5.
127. "Theories about the origin of language". **Hongkong Standard (Education)** 16 June 1989, p.5.
128. "Lessons from evolution". **Hongkong Standard (Education)** 23 June 1989, p.5.
129. (with T.J. Taylor) *Landmarks in Linguistic Thought: the Western Tradition from Socrates to Saussure*. London: Routledge, 1989. xviii + 199 pp. (Routledge history of linguistic thought series)
130. "Degree-0 explanation". **Behavioral and Brain Sciences** 1989, 12:2, pp.344-345.
131. Review of R. Schleifer, *A.J. Greimas and the Nature of Meaning: Linguistics, Semiotics and Discourse Theory*. **Review of English Studies** 1989, 40:160, pp.541-542.
132. "How does writing restructure thought?". **Language & Communication** 1989, 9:2-3, pp.99-106. Reprinted in Roy Harris and George Wolf (eds.). *Integrational Linguistics: a First Reader*. Oxford: Pergamon, 1998. pp.252-261.
133. "English fights for survival in Hong Kong schools". **Hongkong Standard (Education)** 1 November 1989, p.5.

134. "Quelques réflexions sur la tyrannie de l'alphabet". C. Sirat, J. Irigoin and E. Poulle (eds.), *L'Ecriture: le cerveau, l'œil et la main*. Turnhout: Brepols, 1990. pp.195-200.
135. "The integrationist critique of orthodox linguistics". M.P.. Jordan (ed.), *The Sixteenth LACUS Forum 1989*. Lake Bluff: L.A.C.U.S., 1990. pp.63-77. Reprinted in Roy Harris and George Wolf (eds.). *Integrational Linguistics: a First Reader*. Oxford: Pergamon, 1998. pp.15-26.
136. "*Lars Porsena* revisited". C. Ricks and L. Michaels (eds.), *The State of the Language*. Berkeley: University of California Press, 1990. pp.411-421.
137. "The scientist as *Homo Loquens*". R. Bhaskar (ed.), *Harré and his Critics*. Oxford: Blackwell, 1990. pp.64-86.
138. "Semantics and its critics". **Hong Kong Papers in Linguistics and Language Teaching** 1990, 13, pp.35-39.
139. "The dialect myth". J.A. Edmondson, C.Feagin and P Mühlhäusler (eds.), *Development and Diversity. Linguistic Variation across Time and Space. A Festschrift for Charles-James N. Bailey*. Dallas: Summer Institute of Linguistics, 1990. pp.3-19. Reprinted in Roy Harris and George Wolf (eds.). *Integrational Linguistics: a First Reader*. Oxford: Pergamon, 1998. pp.83-95.
140. "Making sense of communicative competence". Nigel Love (ed.), *The Foundations of Linguistic Theory. Selected Writings of Roy Harris*. London: Routledge, 1990. pp.112-135. Reprinted in Roy Harris and George Wolf (eds.). *Integrational Linguistics: a First Reader*. Oxford: Pergamon, 1998. pp.27-45.
141. *The Foundations of Linguistic Theory. Selected Writings of Roy Harris*. Edited by Nigel Love. London: Routledge, 1990. xv + 236 pp.
Contents:
Roy Harris: A chronological bibliography.
Editor's introduction.
Synonymy and morphological analysis.

Words and word criteria in French.
Semantics and translation.
Performative paradigms.
Semantics, performatives and truth.
Truth-conditional semantics and natural languages.
Making sense of communicative competence.
Communication and language.
The spech-communication model in twentieth-century linguistics and its sources.
Must monkeys mean?
Scriptism.
Language as social interaction: integrationalism versus segregationalism.
The semiology of textualization.

142. "On 'Folk' and 'Scientific' linguistic beliefs". S.L.Tsohatzidis (ed.), *Meanings and Prototypes. Studies in Linguistic Categorization.* London: Routledge, 1990. pp.449-464.
143. "On redefining linguistics". Hayley G. Davis and Talbot J. Taylor (eds.), *Redefining Linguistics.* London: Routledge, 1990. pp.18-52.
144. "On freedom of speech". John E. Joseph and Talbot J. Taylor (eds.), *Ideologies of Language.* London: Routledge, 1990. pp.153-161.
145. Review of M. Johnson, *Attribute-Value Logic and the Theory of Grammar.* **History and Philosophy of Logic** 1990, 11, pp.252-253.
146. (with T.J. Taylor) "A second decade for *Language & Communication*". **Language & Communication** 1991, 11:1-2, p.1.
147. Review of J.R. de J. Jackson, *Historical Criticism and the Meaning of Texts.* **Review of English Studies** 1991, 42:166, pp.301-302.
148. Review of A. Rai, *Orwell and the Politics of Despair.* **Review of English Studies** 1991, 42:166, p.307.

149. "Words, which go together. Are languages really fixed or error-free?". Review of Zellig Harris, *A Theory of Language and Information*. **Times Literary Supplement**, 26 July 1991, p.24.
150. "Hobgoblins of a cold warrior". Review of Noam Chomsky, *Deterring Democracy*. **The Independent** 7 September 1991, p.29.
151. Review of J. DeFrancis, *Visible Speech: The Diverse Oneness of Writing Systems*. **Journal of Language and Social Psychology** 1991, 10:3, pp.217-220.
152. "Language". J.W. Yolton, R. Porter and B.M. Stafford (eds.), *The Blackwell Companion to the Enlightenment*. Oxford: Blackwell, 1991. pp.272-274.
153. (editor, with M. Chan) *Asian Voices in English*. Hong Kong: Hong Kong University Press, 1991.
154. (with M. Chan) "Introduction". M. Chan and Roy Harris (eds.), *Asian Voices in English*. Hong Kong: Hong Kong University Press, 1991. pp.1-2.
155. "English versus Islam: the Asian Voice of Salman Rushdie". M. Chan and Roy Harris (eds.), *Asian Voices in English*. Hong Kong: Hong Kong University Press, 1991. pp.87-100.
156. "On scientific method in linguistics". George Wolf (ed.), *New Departures in Linguistics*. New York: Garland, 1992. pp.1-26.
157. "Writing and proto-writing: from sign to metasign". George Wolf (ed.), *New Departures in Linguistics*. New York: Garland, 1992. pp.180-192. Reprinted in Roy Harris and George Wolf (eds.). *Integrational Linguistics: a First Reader*. Oxford: Pergamon, 1998. pp.261-269.
158. "Ecriture et notation". C. Pontecorvo and C. Blanche-Benveniste (eds.), *Proceedings of the Workshop on Orality versus Literacy: Concepts, Methods and Data*. Strasbourg: European Science Foundation, 1993. pp.9-42.

159. "Saussure and linguistic geography". *Language Sciences* 1993, 8:1, pp.1-14.
160. "Another Crystal maze". Review of David Crystal, *An Encyclopedic Dictionary of Language and Languages*. **Times Literary Supplement** 16 April 1993, p.10.
161. "Signs and sentences". Review of Y. Tobin, *Semiotics and Linguistics*. *Semiotica* 1993, 95:1-2, pp.141-146.
162. "Three models of signification". H.S. Gill (ed.), *Structures of Signification*. New Delhi: Wiley, 1993. 3, pp.665-677. Reprinted in Roy Harris and George Wolf (eds.). *Integrational Linguistics: a First Reader*. Oxford: Pergamon, 1998. pp.113-125.
163. "Introduction" to Adam Smith's *Considerations Concerning the First Formation of Languages. British Linguistics in the Eighteenth Century*. London: Routledge/Thoemmes, 1993.
164. "Introduction" to James Beattie's *The Theory of Language. British Linguistics in the Eighteenth Century*. London: Routledge/Thoemmes, 1993. pp. v-xii.
165. "Introduction" to James Harris's *Hermes. British Linguistics in the Eighteenth Century*. London: Routledge/Thoemmes, 1993. pp. v-xi.
166. "Introduction" to John Horne Tooke's *Diversions of Purley. British Linguistics in the Eighteenth Century*. London: Routledge/Thoemmes, 1993. pp. v-xii.
167. "Introduction" to Joseph Priestley's *Lectures on the Theory of Language and Universal Grammar. British Linguistics in the Eighteenth Century*. London: Routledge/Thoemmes, 1993. pp. v-xi.
168. "Introduction" to William Jones' *Discourses Delivered at the Asiatic Society 1785-1792. British Linguistics in the Eighteenth Century*. London: Routledge/Thoemmes, 1993. pp. v-xi.

169. "Integrational linguistics." *Actes du XVe Congrès International des Linguistes*. Sainte-Foy: Presses de l'Université Laval, 1993. v.1, pp.321-323.
170. "Linguistic questions that linguistics does not ask". *Actes du XVe Congrès International des Linguistes*. Sainte-Foy: Presses de l'Université Laval, 1993. v.4, pp.243-246.
171. (editor and translator with E. Komatsu) Ferdinand de Saussure. *Troisième Cours de Linguistique Générale (1910-1911)*. Oxford: Pergamon, 1993.
172. (editor, with Rom Harré) *Linguistics and Philosophy. The Controversial Interface*. Oxford: Pergamon, 1993.
173. (with Rom Harré) "Preface". Rom Harré and Roy Harris (eds.), *Linguistics and Philosophy. The Controversial Interface*. Oxford: Pergamon, 1993. pp.ix-xi.
174. "What is philosophy of linguistics?". Rom Harré and Roy Harris (eds.), *Linguistics and Philosophy. The Controversial Interface*. Oxford: Pergamon, 1993. pp.3-19.
175. "Saussure, Wittgenstein and *la règle du jeu*". Rom Harré and Roy Harris (eds.), *Linguistics and Philosophy. The Controversial Interface*. Oxford: Pergamon, 1993. pp.219-231.
176. "Graphically speaking". Review of T. Conley, *The Graphic Unconscious in Early Modern French Writing*. **Times Literary Supplement** 24 September 1993, p.11.
177. "Criticizing Saussure". Review of D. Holdcroft, *Saussure: Signs, System and Arbitrariness*. **Semiotica** 1994, 98:1-2, pp.181-186.
178. *La sémiologie de l'écriture*. Paris: CNRS, 1994 [c1993]. 376 pp.
179. "Introduction" to Alexander Murray's *History of the European Languages. British Linguistics in the Nineteenth Century*. London: Routledge/Thoemmes, 1994. pp.v-xi.
180. "Introduction" to excerpts from works by Dugald Stewart, Nicholas Wiseman, Robert Chambers, Charles Darwin and Henry Sweet's *History of Language. British*

Linguistics in the Nineteenth Century. London: Routledge/Thoemmes, 1994. pp.vii-xiii.
181. "Introduction" to Max Müller's *Lectures on the Science of Language. British Linguistics in the Nineteenth Century*. London: Routledge/Thoemmes, 1994. pp.v-x.
182. "Introduction" to Richard Chenevix Trench's *On the Study of Words. British Linguistics in the Nineteenth Century*. London: Routledge/Thoemmes, 1994. pp.v-xi.
183. "Introduction" to William Dwight Whitney's *The Life and Growth of Language. British Linguistics in the Nineteenth Century*. London: Routledge/Thoemmes, 1994. pp.v-xi.
184. "Semiotic aspects of writing". H. Günther and O. Ludwig (eds.), *Schrift und Schriftlichkeit*. Berlin: De Gruyter, 1994. v.1, pp.41-48.
185. "Talking pictures (no vision needed)". Review of W.J.T. Mitchell, *Picture Theory*. **Times Higher Education Supplement** 6 January 1995, p.22.
186. "A well-defined corpus". Review of J. Willinsky, *Empire of Words: The Reign of the OED*. **Times Higher Education Supplement** 14 April 1995, p.29.
187. "Opening the door to language". Review of R.E. Asher and J.M.Y. Simpson (eds.), *The Encyclopedia of Language and Linguistics*. **Times Literary Supplement** 21 April 1995, pp.10-11.
188. "Translating MITspeak". Review of S. Pinker, *The Language Instinct. How the Mind Creates Language*. **Essays in Criticism** 1995, 45:3 pp.272-279.
189. "Introduction" *The Wellesley Series. Nineteenth Century Sources in the Humanities and Social Sciences. I. Language and Linguistics*. 4 volumes. London: Routledge/thoemmes, 1995. v.1, vii-x.
190. "Put that in your pipe and smoke it". Review of F. Merrell, *Semiosis in the Postmodern Age*. **Times Higher Education Supplement** 22 September 1995, p.21.

191. "The lesson to learn from Ern". Review of J. Harwood, *Eliot to Derrida: the Poverty of Interpretation* and N. Royle, *After Derrida*. **Times Higher Education Supplement** 13 October 1995, p.22.
192. "Saussure, generative grammar and integrational linguistics". T. De Mauro and S. Sugeta (eds.), *Saussure and Linguistics Today*. Roma: Bulzoni, 1995. pp.203-213.
193. *Signs of Writing*, London: Routledge, 1995 [i.e. 1996], vii + 185pp.
194. "What a load of cratylisme". Review of G. Genette, *Mimologics*, trans. T.E. Morgan. **Times Higher Education Supplement**, 15 March 1996, p. 21.
195. "Introduction" to *The Origin of Language*, Bristol: Thoemmes Press, 1996, pp. vii–xii.
196. Review of R. Bradford, *A Linguistic History of English Poetry*, **Review of English Studies**, 1996 47:186, pp.222-223.
197. "To ceramise or not to ceramise", **Studio Pottery**, 1996, 21 (June/July), p.4.
198. *The Language Connection. Philosophy and Linguistics*, Bristol: Thoemmes Press, 1996, xix + 193pp.
199. "Fluent Flemings flummox xenophobes". Review of J. Green, *Chasing the Sun: Dictionary-Makers and the Dictionaries they Made*. **Times Higher Education Supplement**, 26 July 1996, p.21.
200. "More usage than abusage". Review of D. Cameron, *Verbal Hygiene*. **Times Higher Education Supplement**, 23 August 1996, p.22.
201. "As easy as a, b, see?" Review of J.-C. Corbeil (Ed.), *The Oxford Visual Dictionary*. **Times Higher Education Supplement**, 13 September 1996, p.27.
202. *Signs, Language and Communication*, London: Routledge, 1996, xii + 279pp.

203. "Prehistoric moving picture show". Review of J. Clottes and J. Courtin, *The Cave Beneath the Sea: Paleolithic Images at Cosquer*, and J.-M. Chauvet, E. Brunel Deschamps and C. Hillaire, *Chauvet Cave: The Discovery of the World's Oldest Paintings*. **Times Higher Education Supplement**, 20 December 1996, pp.19-20.
204. "Writing and notation". H. Günther and O. Ludwig (eds.) *Schrift und Schriftlichkeit*. Berlin: de Gruyter, 1996, v.2, pp.1559-1568.
205. "From an integrational point of view". George Wolf and Nigel Love (eds.), *Linguistics Inside Out: Roy Harris and His Critics*. (Amsterdam Studies in the Theory and History of Linguistic Science, vol. 148) Amsterdam-Philadelphia: John Benjamins, 1997, pp.229-310.
206. "Nero's kind of fiddler". Review of J. Collins and B. Mayblin, *Derrida for Beginners*. **Times Higher Education Supplement**, 31 January 1997, p.24.
207. "The writing revolution: grammatology and the computer", **Technos** 1997, 6:2, pp.33-36.
208. "Fiddle, fiddle, fiddle". Review of J. Collins and B. Mayblin, *Derrida for Beginners*. **Times Literary Supplement** 21 March 1997
209. "Symbol-minded". Review of R. Sassoon and A. Gaur, *Signs, Symbols and Icons: Prehistory to the Computer Age*, and P. Mollerup, *Marks of Excellence: The History and Taxonomy of Trademarks*. **Times Higher Education Supplement**, 30 May 1997, p.20.
210. (with T.J. Taylor) *Landmarks in Linguistic Thought. The Western Tradition from Socrates to Saussure*. 2nd Edition. London: Routledge, 1997, xxi + 234pp.
211. "Le Néron de la philosophie". [Trad. Béatrice Vierne] Review of J. Collins and B. Mayblin, *Derrida for Beginners*. **Le Lecteur**, 1997 Juillet/Août 98, p. 9.

212. "Why two plus two can equal one". Review of D.R. Olson and N. Torrance (eds.), *Modes of Thought: Explorations in Culture and Cognition*. **Times Higher Education Supplement**, 1 July 1997, p.25.
213. "Fighting the many enemies". Review of M. Proffitt (ed.), *Oxford English Dictionary Additions Series Vol. 3* and J. Honey, *Language is Power: the Story of Standard English and its Enemies*. **Times Higher Education Supplement**, 5 September 1997, p. 19.
214. (with T.J. Taylor) 言語論のランドマーク：ソクラテスからソシュールまで / ロイ・ハリス,タルボット・J・テイラー 共著 ; 斎藤伸治,滝沢直宏 共訳. 東京 : 大修館書店, 1997. [*Gengoron no randomaku: Sokuratesu kara Soshuru made*. Roi Harisu, Tarubotto J. Teira kyocho; Saito Shinji, Takizawa Naohiro kyoyaku. Japanese translation of the 1st edition of *Landmarks in Linguistic Thought. The Western Tradition from Socrates to Saussure*. Translators, Naohiro Takizawa and Shinji Saito. Tokyo: Taishukan, 1997] viii + 349pp.
215. "Pillowtalk for cavemen". Review of T.W. Deacon, *The Symbolic Species: The Co-evolution of Language and the Human Brain*. **Times Higher Education Supplement**, 7 November 1997, p.20.
216. "Jakobson's Saussure". *Acta Linguistica Hafniensia*, 1997, 29, pp.75-88. Reprinted in John E. Joseph (ed.), *Ferdinand de Saussure. Vol. 2: The Course in General Linguistics and its Early Impact* London and New York: Routledge, 2013. (Critical Assessments of Leading Linguists series) pp.133-145; and in Margaret Thomas (ed.), *Roman Jakobson*. London and New York: Routledge, 2014. (Critical Assessments of Leading Linguists) pp. 435-447.

217. "How can language float in a cultural vacuum?" Review of M. Toolan, *Total Speech* and J.J. Gumperz and S.C. Levinson (Eds.), *Rethinking Linguistic Relativity*. **Times Literary Supplement**, 26 December 1997, p.27.
218. "What did Saussure mean by signification?" L. Lapierre, I.Oore and H.R. Hunte (eds.), *Mélanges de linguistique offerts à Rostislav Kocourek*. Halifax, N.S., Presses d'ALFA, 1997. pp.271-276.
219. "A few image problems". Review of D. Lopes, *Understanding Pictures*. **Times Higher Education Supplement**, 30 January 1998, p.30.
220. "Defining the undefinable". Review of F. Coulmas (ed.), *The Handbook of Sociolinguistics*. **Times Higher Education Supplement**, 27 February 1998, p.37.
221. "A fine romance". Review of R. Posner, *The Romance Languages*. **Times Literary Supplement**, 17 April 1998, pp.30-31.
222. "Signs of omission". Review of P.V. Lamarque (ed.), *Concise Encyclopedia of Philosophy of Language*. **Times Higher Education Supplement**, 1 May 1998, p.27.
223. "Théorie de l'écriture: une approche intégrationnelle". J.-G. Lapacherie (ed.), *Propriétés de l'écriture*. Pau: P.U.P, 1998. pp.15-17.
224. "Autonomie/intégration/écriture: littératie?" J.-G. Lapacherie (ed.), *Propriétés de l'écriture*. Pau: P.U.P., 1998. pp.81-82.
225. "Good maths, stale grammar". Review of R.G. Heck, Jnr. (ed.), *Language, Thought and Logic: Essays in Honour of Michael Dummett*. **Times Higher Education Supplement**, 9 October 1998, p.26.
226. Review of P.A.M. Seuren, *Western Linguistics. An Historical Introduction*. **Times Literary Supplement**, 23 October 1998, p.37.

227. *Introduction to Integrational Linguistics*. Oxford: Pergamon, 1998. xi + 168pp.
228. (editor, with George Wolf). *Integrational Linguistics: a First Reader*. Oxford: Pergamon, 1998. vii + 360pp.
229. *L'origine della scrittura*. Rev. ed. of *The Origin of Writing*. Trans. Antonio Perri. Viterbo: Nuovi Equilibri, 1998. 191pp.
230. "Integrational linguistics and the structuralist legacy". B. Caron (ed.), *Proceedings of the XVIth International Congress of Linguists*, Oxford, Elsevier, 1998. CD p.508.
231. "Integrational linguistics and the structuralist legacy". *Language & Communication*, 1999, 19:1, pp.45-68. Reprinted in: Paul Cobley (ed.), *Communication Theories: Critical Concepts in Media and Cultural Studies*. London and New York: Routledge, 2006., v.2, pp.125-151.
232. Review of A. Dalby, *Dictionary of Languages*. **Times Literary Supplement**, 5 February 1999, pp.30-31.
233. "Missing the writing on the wall". Review of R. Keller, *A Theory of Linguistic Signs*. **Times Higher Education Supplement**, 5 March 1999, p.30.
234. "What's the big idea? The story of conceptual art". ***Artists & Illustrators***, 1999, 152 (May), pp.44-45.
235. *Signos de escritura*. Trans. Patricia Willson. Barcelona: Gedisa, 1999. 253pp. (Trans. of *Signs of Writing.*)
236. "Babel and psychobabble". Review of G.T.M. Altmann, *The Ascent of Babel: An Exploration of Language, Mind and Understanding*. **Times Higher Education Supplement**, 7 May 1999, p.35.
237. "Mystic muddles". Review of U. Eco, *Serendipities. Language and Lunacy*. **Times Literary Supplement**, 11 June 1999, p.26.
238. "Look who's talking now". Review of S. Savage-Rumbaugh, S.G. Shanker and T.J. Taylor, *Apes, Language*

and the Human Mind. ***Times Higher Education Supplement***, 9 July 1999, p.27.
239. "Hit and myth: Barthes's inglorious life and times". Review of A. Stafford, *Roland Barthes, Phenomenon and Myth: An Intellectual Biography*. ***Times Higher Education Supplement***, 20 August 1999, p.24.
240. "Deepening the Derridean fog". Review of C. Howells, *Derrida: Deconstruction from Phenomenology to Ethics*. ***Times Higher Education Supplement***, 8 October 1999, p.28.
241. "Gulliver and the semioticians". H.S. Gill and G. Manetti (eds.), *Signs and Signification*, v.2 (special issue of ***Language Forum*** 26:1-2). New Delhi, Bahri, 2000. pp.191-199.
242. "Abundant signs of confusion". Review of P. Boissac (ed.), *Encyclopedia of Semiotics*. ***Times Higher Education Supplement***, 11 February 2000, p.28.
243. "On the tyranny of the alphabet". Review of W. Bright (ed.), *Written Language and Literacy*, Nos. *1–3*. ***Times Higher Education Supplement***, 14 April 2000, p.31.
244. "Reflections on a real character". R.E. Asher and Roy Harris (eds.), *Linguisticoliterary*, Delhi, Pilgrims, 2000. pp.225-235.
245. "What's the code for 'We've heard this one before'?" Review of E. de Bono, *The de Bono Code Book: Going Beyond the Limits of Language*. ***Times Higher Education Supplement***, 18 August 2000, p.26.
246. *Rethinking Writing*, London: Athlone, 2000. xvi + 254pp.
247. "Saussure for all seasons". Review of P.J. Thibault, *Re-reading Saussure*. ***Semiotica***, 2000, 131:3/4, pp.273-287.
248. "Identities, differences, and analogies: the problem Saussure could not solve". ***Historiographica Linguistica***, 2000, 27:2/3, pp.297-305. Reprinted in John E. Joseph (ed.),

Ferdinand de Saussure. Vol. 2: The Course in General Linguistics and its Early Impact. London and New York: Routledge, 2013. (Critical Assessments of Leading Linguists) pp.77-84.
249. *Saussure and his Interpreters*, Edinburgh: Edinburgh University Press, 2001. vii + 224pp.
250. "Comment: 'How an Andean 'writing without words' works'". *Current Anthropology*, 2001, 42:1, pp.21-22.
251. "Genesis and high gossip". Review of George Steiner, *Grammars of Creation*. **Times Higher Education Supplement**, 4 May 2001, p.27.
252. "A few Blair babes but not a lot of mickle". Review of Elizabeths Knowles (ed.), *The Oxford Dictionary of Phrase and Fable*. **Times Higher Education Supplement**, 2 November 2001, p.26.
253. 'Rethinking writing'. S. Covino (ed.), *La Scrittura Professionale: ricerca, prassi, insegnamento : atti del I Convegno di studi : Perugia, Università per Stranieri, 23-25 ottobre 2000*. Roma: Olschki, 2001. pp.53-61.
254. "A note on the linguistics of environmentalism". A. Fill and P. Mühlhäusler (eds.), *The Ecolinguistics Reader. Language, Ecology and the Environment*. London: Continuum, 2001. pp.154-158.
255. "Linguistics after Saussure". Paul Cobley (ed.), *The Routledge Companion to Semiotics and Linguistics*. London: Routledge, 2001. pp.118-133.
256. Entries for 'Aristotle', 'Augustine', 'Binarism', 'Distinctive Feature', 'Humboldt', 'Langage', 'Langue', 'Parole', 'Philology', 'Port-Royal', 'Saussure', 'Semiology', 'Signified', 'Signifier', 'Synchrony (Synchronic)', 'Syntagm, Syntagmatic', and 'Value'. Paul Cobley (ed.), *The Routledge Companion to Semiotics and Linguistics*. London: Routledge, 2001.

257. "Preface". Roy Harris (ed.), *The Language Myth in Western Culture*. London: Curzon, 2002. p.vii.
258. "The role of the language myth in the Western cultural tradition". Roy Harris (ed.), *The Language Myth in Western Culture*. London: Curzon, 2002. pp.1-24.
259. "Looking in for the meaning without". Review of Ray Jackendoff, *Foundations of Language: Brain, Meaning, Grammar, Evolution*. **Times Higher Education Supplement**, 15 February 2002, p.27.
260. "Language: black, white and shades of gray". Piers Gray, *Stalin on Linguistics and Other Essays*, Ed. C. MacCabe and V. Rothschild. Basingstoke: Palgrave, 2002. pp.258-260.
261. "Why words really do not stay still". Review of F. de Saussure, *Écrits de linguistique générale*, Ed. S. Bouquet and R. Engler. **Times Literary Supplement**, 26 July 2002, p.30.
262. "Sideswipe with blinkered eyes". Review of Alan Fletcher, *The Art of Looking Sideways*. **Times Higher Education Supplement,** 9 August 2002, p.25.
263. "On redefining linguistics". H.G. Davis & T.J. Taylor (eds.), *Rethinking Linguistics*. London: RoutledgeCurzon, 2002. pp.17-68.
264. "Nagarjuna, Heracleitus and the problem of language". H.G. Davis & T.J. Taylor (eds.), *Rethinking Linguistics*. London: RoutledgeCurzon, 2002. pp.171-188.
265. "Fuzzy theories and daft expressions". Review of P. Hobson, *The Cradle of Thought*. **Times Higher Education Supplement**, 4 October 2002, p.31.
266. "English: how not to teach it". **The European English Messenger**, 2002, 11:2, pp.57-61.

267. "Is language speech?" Review of T. Jansen, Speak and J.H. McWhorter, *The Power of Babel*. **Times Literary Supplement**, 18 October 2002, p.36.
268. "Lashed into line by grim grammarians". Review of A. Bierce, *The Devil's Dictionary*; W. Cobbett, *Grammar of the English Language*; H. Fowler, *A Dictionary of Modern English Usage*: H. and F. Fowler, *The King's English*; R. Burchfield, *The English Language*; N. Mitford (Ed.) *Noblesse Oblige*. Reprints in the Oxford Language Classics series. **Times Higher Education Supplement**, 29 November 2002. Textbook Guide p. x.
269. "Literacy and the future of writing: An integrational perspective". J. Brockmeier, M. Wang and D.R. Olson (eds.), *Literacy, Narrative and Culture*. London: Curzon, 2002. pp.35-51.
270. "L'écriture: pierre d'achoppement pour la sémiologie saussurienne". S. Bouquet (ed.), *Ferdinand de Saussure*. Paris: L'Herne, 2003. pp.228-233.
271. *The Necessity of Artspeak. The language of the arts in the Western tradition*, London: Continuum, 2003. xvii + 222pp.
272. "Some things never change". Review of W. Ayres-Bennett and R. Sampson (eds.), *Interpreting the History of French*. **Times Literary Supplement**, 11 April 2003, p.32.
273. Review of Ferdinand de Saussure, *Écrits de linguistique générale*, S. Bouquet et R. Engler (eds.), Paris: Gallimard. **Recherches Sémiotiques**, 2003, 23, pp.247-252.
274. *History, Science and the Limits of Language. An Integrationist Approach*, Shimla: Indian Institute of Advanced Study, 2003. 87pp.
275. *La tirannia dell'alfabeto. Ripensare la scrittura*. Trans. Antonio Perri. Viterbo: Stampa Alternativa & Graffiti, 2003. 275pp. (Trans. of *Rethinking Writing*.)

276. "Why false teeth make Jesus an only child". Review of J. Weightman, *The Cat Sat on the Mat: Language and the Absurd*. **Times Higher Education Supplement**, 10 October 2003, p.33.
277. "Introduction du traducteur". Trans. by C.S. Forel of Introduction to F. de Saussure, *Course in General Linguistics* (1983). **Cahiers Ferdinand de Saussure**, 2003, 53, pp.345-353.
278. "Post-scriptum du traducteur", **Cahiers Ferdinand de Saussure**, 2003, 53, pp. 353-355.
279. *Saussure and his Interpreters*, 2nd Ed. Edinburgh: Edinburgh University Press, 2003. xi + 262pp.
280. 'Wall papers'. Review of J. Webster (Ed.), *The Collected Works of M.A.K. Halliday*, vols 1–3, **Times Literary Supplement**, 9 January 2004, p. 11.
281. 'A warning to students'. **Times Literary Supplement**, 30 January 2004, p. 13.
282. *The Linguistics of History*, Edinburgh, Edinburgh University Press, 2004. xi + 244pp.
283. 'Stale words on the way we speak'. Review of *Everyday Language and Everyday Life* by Richard Hoggart, **Times Higher Education Supplement**, 23 July 2004, p. 28.
284. 'Integrationism, language, mind and world'. **Language Sciences**, 2004, 26: 6, pp. 727–739.
285. 'Latin on the rise'. Review of *Languages and Communities in Early Modern Europe* by Peter Burke, **Times Literary Supplement**, 24 December 2004, p. 42.
286. 'Big sister's big rebuff'. **Times Higher Education Supplement**, 21 January 2005, p. 14.
287. 'Bit of this (or that) for you (or I)'. Review *of Reflecting the Mind: Indexicality and Quasi-Indexicality* by Eros Corazza, **Times Higher Education Supplement**, 8 April 2005, p. 27.

288. 'Anyone familiar with the phrase 'caveat emptor'?' Review of *A Natural History of Latin* by Tore Janson, **Times Higher Education Supplement**, 15 July 2005, p. 24.
289. *The Semantics of Science*, London, Continuum, 2005. xvi + 219 pp.
290. 'Schrift und linguistische Theorie'. In G. Grube, W. Kogge and S. Krämer (Eds.), *Schrift. Kulturtechnik zwischen Auge, Hand und Maschine*, Munich, Fink, 2005, pp. 61–80.
291. 'Speaking out for the right to speak evil'. **Times Higher Education Supplement**, 9 December 2005, p. 14.
292. 'First words'. Review of *The Unfolding of Language* by Guy Deutscher, and *Language Origins*, Ed. M. Tallerman, **Times Literary Supplement**, 6 January 2006, p. 24.
293. *Integrationist Notes and Papers 2003–2005*, Crediton, Tree Tongue, 2006. 73 pp.

Contents:

1. Communication: or How Jill Got Her Apple.
2. English: How Not To Teach It.
3. Texts and Contexts.
4. On Indeterminacy.
5. Time, Language and Angels.
6. Synchrony and Diachrony.
7. Integrationism and Philosophy of Language.
8. On Determinacy of Linguistic Form.
9. Integrationism and Arbitrariness.
10. Integrationism and Etymology.
11. Signs and Stories.
12. Meaning and Experience.
13. On Holistic Models of Language.
14. Integrationism and the Foundations of Mathematics.
15. Integrationism and Godspeak.

294. 'Integrational linguistics and semiology'. In K. Brown (Ed.), *The Encyclopedia of Language and Linguistics*, 2nd edn, Oxford, Elsevier, 2006, Vol.5, pp. 714–718.
295. 'Modern Linguistics: 1800 to the present day'. In K. Brown (Ed.), *The Encyclopedia of Language and Linguistics*, 2nd edn, Oxford, Elsevier, 2006, Vol.8, pp. 203–210.
296. 'Western linguistic thought before 1800'. In K. Brown (Ed.), *The Encyclopedia of Language and Linguistics*, 2nd edn., Oxford, Elsevier, 2006, Vol.13, pp. 559–571.
297. 'History and comparative philology'. In N. Love (Ed.), *Language and History. Integrationist perspectives*, London, Routledge, 2006, pp. 41–59.
298. 'How to make history with words'. In N.Love (Ed.), *Language and History. Integrationist perspectives*, London, Routledge, 2006, pp. 142–155.
299. 'Linguistics and philosophy'. In A. Grayling, A. Pyle and N. Goulder (Eds.), *The Continuum Encyclopedia of British Philosophy*, London, Thoemmes Continuum, 2006, vol. 3, pp. 1894–1902.
300. 'Meaning'. In A. Grayling, A. Pyle and N. Goulder (Eds.), *The Continuum Encyclopedia of British Philosophy*, London, Thoemmes Continuum, 2006, vol. 3, pp. 2129–2130.
301. 'Ordinary language philosophy'. In A. Grayling, A. Pyle and N. Goulder (Eds.), *The Continuum Encyclopedia of British Philosophy*, 2006, vol.3, pp. 2384–2385.
302. 'Was Saussure an integrationist?' In L. de Saussure (Ed.), *Nouveaux regards sur Saussure. Mélanges offerts à René Amacker*, Genève, Droz, 2006, pp. 209–217.
303. 'Want to talk? First show me your credentials'. **Times Higher Education Supplement**, 29 September 2006, p. 12.

304. 'Visuelle und verbale Mehrdeutigkeit – oder Warum ceci niemals eine Pfeife war'. Tr. J.G. Schneider. *Sprache und Literatur*, 2006, 98, pp. 77–91.
305. 'The grammar'. Review of vols. 4–7 in *The Collected Works of M.A.K. Halliday*, Ed. J. Webster. *Times Literary Supplement*, 17 November 2006, p. 31.
306. 'Defending literature'. Review of D. Schalkwyk, *Literature and the Touch of the Real*. *Language Sciences*, 2007, vol. 29, No. 1, pp. 109–114.
307. 'Exactly what is it that we cannot say?' Review of K. Allan and K. Burridge, *Forbidden Words: Taboo and the Censoring of Language*. *Times Higher Education Supplement*, 9 February 2007, p. 26.
308. 'Mother tongue twisted by drive for global gains'. *Times Higher Education Supplement*, 30 March 2007, p. 12.
309. 'Walk on wild side reveals colour but not clarity'. Review of J. Attlee, *Isolarion: a Different Oxford Journey*. *Times Higher Education Supplement*, 6 Aprl 2007, p. 22.
310. (with C.M. Hutton) *Definition in Theory and Practice. Language, Lexicography and the Law*. London: Continuum, 2007. 238pp.
311. 'Ewe, Welsh? Baa Humbug'. Review of D. Crystal, *By Hook or by Crook: a Journey in Search of English*. *Times Higher Education Supplement*, 29 June 2007, p. 22.
312. 'Concepts where there are none'. Review of J.R. Hurford, *The Origins of Meaning: Language in the Light of Evolution*. *Times Higher Education Supplement*, 26 October 2007, p. 24.
313. 'Integrational linguistics'. In *Handbook of Pragmatics*, Ed. J. Verschueren and J-O. Östman. Amsterdam: Benjamins, 2007.

314. 'Ferdinand de Saussure'. In *Handbook of Pragmatics*, Ed. J. Verschueren and J-O. Östman. Amsterdam: Benjamins, 2007.
315. 'Defining the undefinable'. *Times Higher Education*, 10 January 2008, p. 20.
316. Review of E. Lucie-Smith, *Censoring the Body* and J. Petley, *Censoring the Word*. *Times Higher Education*, 31 January 2008, pp. 50-51.
317. 'Barbarous scratchings or universal system? The Chinese puzzle on paper'. *Times Higher Education*, 7 February 2008, pp. 26–27.
318. 'Die integrationale Zeichenkonzeption'. Tr. J.G. Schneider, *Zeitschrift für Semiotik* 2008, 30: 1–2, pp. 11–28.
319. 'The decline of reason'. *Times Higher Education*, 15 May 2008, pp. 40–42.
320. Review of Luce Irigaray, *Sharing the World*. *Times Higher Education*, 17 August 2008, p. 50.
321. 'A song and dance about Western values'. *Times Higher Education*, 28 August 2008, pp. 36–39.
322. *Mindboggling. Preliminaries to a science of the mind*. Luton, Pantaneto Press, 2008. ix + 173pp.
323. 'In the beginning was the letter'. Review of Brian Rotman, *Becoming Beside Ourselves: The Alphabet, Ghosts and Distributed Human Being*. *Times Higher Education*, 20 November 2008, p. 50.
324. 'Logic, arbitrariness and Saussurean linguistics'. In Michel Arrivé (Ed.), *Du côté de chez Saussure*, Limoges, Lambert-Lucas, 2008, pp. 151–164.
325. 'Implicit and explicit language teaching'. In Michael Toolan (Ed.), *Language Teaching. Integrational Linguistic Approaches,* New York, Routledge, 2009, pp. 24–46.

326. *Rationality and the Literate Mind*, New York, Routledge, 2009. xv + 190pp.
327. 'Freedom and hypocrisy'. Speech at the May 20, 2009 International Academic Freedom Day seminar. Available on the Times Higher Education website as a related file for the article by Rebecca Attwood 'Freedom fighters 'when it suits'', May 28, 2009: http://www.timeshighereducation.co.uk/story.asp?storycode=406716
328. *Integrationist Notes and Papers 2006–2008*, Gamlingay, Bright Pen, 2009. v + 85 pp.
Contents:
16. Integrating Freud.
17. Freud and the Language Myth.
18. Integrating Autism.
19. The Grammar of Numbers.
20. Getting at the Truth.
21. Words Most Wonderful.
22. What a Linguistic Fact is Not.
23. The Myth of Reference.
24. Integrating Husserl.
25. The Integrational Conception of the Sign.
329. 'Speech and writing'. In D.R. Olson and N. Torrance (Eds.), *The Cambridge Handbook of Literacy*, Cambridge, Cambridge University Press, 2009, pp. 46–58.
330. '*Cours de linguistique générale*. By Ferdinand de Saussure', **Times Higher Education**, 3 April 2009, p. 42.
331. *After Epistemology*, Gamlingay, Bright Pen, 2009. vi + 187pp.
332. Entries for 'Aristotle', 'Augustine', 'Binarism', 'Humboldt', 'Langage', 'Langue', 'Paradigm (Paradigmatic)', 'Parole', 'Philology', 'Port-Royal', 'Saussure', 'Semiology', 'Synchrony (Synchronic)',

'Syntagm (Syntagmatic)', and 'Value'. In *The Routledge Companion to Semiotics*, Ed. Paul Cobley, London, Routledge. (The book is dated 2010 but was released in July 2009).

333. 'Reassessing Russell'. Review of K. Green, *Bertrand Russell, Language and Linguistic Theory*, London, Continuum, 2007. **Language Sciences** 2010, 32, pp. 143–148.

334. *The Great Debate About Art*, Chicago: Prickly Paradigm Press, 2010. iii + 134pp.

335. 'Wittgenstein on 'primitive' languages'. In V. Munz, K. Puhl and J. Wang, *Language and World Part One: Essays on the Philosophy of Wittgenstein*, Heusenstamm: Ontos Verlag, 2010, p. 243-263.

336. (interviewed by Marc Haas). "'The question is not whether integrationism can survive outside linguistics, but whether linguistics can survive outside integrationism': an Interview with Roy Harris". **Language Sciences** July 2011, 33:4, pp.498-502.

337. *Integrationist Notes and Papers 2009-2011*. Gamlingay: Bright Pen, Authors OnLine, 2011. iv + 104 pp.

Contents:

26. Language Myths, East and West
27. On 'Primitive' Languages in Linguistic Theory
28. Linguistic Relativity
29. Saussure and Logic
30. Sentences and Systems
31. Theory of Mind
32. Mental Misrepresentations
33. The Quest for Qualia
34. The Translation Myth
35. On Ultimate Questions

338. *Integrationist Notes and Papers 2012*. Gamlingay: Bright Pen, Authors OnLine, 2012. v + 103 pp.
Contents:
36. Russell Revisited
37. Minds, Brains and Language Machines
38. Logic and Babel
39. Reason and Truth
40. Laws of Thought
41. Ordinary Language
42. Forms of Talk and Forms of Action
43. By Any Other Name
44. Any Questions?
339. *Integrating Reality*. Gamlingay: Bright Pen, Authors OnLine, 2012. vi + 141 pp.
340. "First language". **Times Literary Supplement** 27 Apr. 2012, nr.5691, pp.9-10.
341. *Language and Intelligence*. Gamlingay: Bright Pen, Authors OnLine, 2012. vi + 141 pp.
342. *Integrationist Notes and Papers 2013*. Gamlingay: Bright Pen, Authors OnLine, 2013. iv + 111pp.
Contents:
45 Ordinary Language Again
46 Empiricism and Linguistics
47 Why There Are No Languages
48 On Relativism
49 Much Ado About Nothing
50 Languages and Politics
51 Normality and Neuroplasticity
343. *Integrationist Notes and Papers 2014*. Gamlingay: Bright Pen, Authors OnLine, 2014. 78 pp.
Contents:
52 On Agreement
53 On Language Acquisition

54 Truth and Objectivity
55 Synchronic/Diachronic
56 On Lexicography
57 Thoughts Immaculate
58 What-Is-It-Like?
59 Doubts and Certainties
60 Questions and Answers

II. Reviews of Books by Roy Harris 1973–2014

SYNONYMY AND LINGUISTIC ANALYSIS (1973)

344. [unsigned] "Semantic similarities". *TLS. Times Literary Supplement* 25 May 1973, nr. 3716, p.591.
345. Edward Robert Maxwell. *Library Journal* 1 June 1973, 98:11, p.1819.
346. Stephen J. Noren. *Philosophy and Phenomenological Research* December 1973, 34:2, p.288.
347. Viktor Raskin. *Philosophia* June 1976, 6:2, pp.377–378.

THE LANGUAGE-MAKERS (1980)

348. Randolph Quirk. "Langage rich of treasures". *The Times* 27 May 1980, p.9.
349. M.J. Wilding. [Letter to the editor]. *The Times* 9 June 1980.
350. N.V. Smith. [Letter to the editor]. *The Times* 14 June 1980.
351. Anthony Burgess. "What's in a word?" *The Observer* (London, England). 15 June 1980, nr. 9851, p.29.
352. T.P. Waldron. "For the want of a theory". *TLS. Times Literary Supplement* 11 July 1980, pp.785-786.
353. G. Gazdar and N. Smith. [Letter to the editor]. *TLS. Times Literary Supplement* 22 August 1980.
354. Barbara Strang. "Language questions". *London Review of Books* 17 July/6 August 1980, 2:14, p.17.
355. John Weightman. "Words, words, words: John Weightman on linguistic theory". *Times Educational Supplement* 8 August 1980, nr. 3347, p.27.
356. F.C. Stork. *British Book News* September 1980, p.528.
357. [unsigned] *CHOICE: Current Reviews for Academic Libraries* November 1980, 18:3, p.390.

358. Jarnes A. McGilvray. *Canadian Philosophical Reviews* October 1981, 1:5, pp.209-212.
359. Marie Louise Pratt. *Language* September 1981, 57:3, pp.698-701.
360. Charles-James N. Bailey. *Arbeitspapiere zur Linguistik* 1981, 12, pp.98-114.
361. John Deigh. *Ethics* January 1983, 2, p.420.

THE LANGUAGE MYTH (1981)

362. Jonathan Lear. "Finding words for ideas". *TLS. Times Literary Supplement* 2 October 1981 p.1130.
363. Geoffrey Sampson. *The Times Higher Education Supplement* 16 October 1981, p.21.
364. David Crystal. "Improvising language". *Listener* 17 October 1981, nr.2727, p.311.
365. Richard L. Street. *The Quarterly Journal of Speech* November 1982, 4, pp.450-451.
366. Michael Dummett. "Linguistics demythologised". *London Review of Books*. 19 August 1982, 4:15, pp. 9-11.
367. [unsigned] *CHOICE: Current Reviews for Academic Libraries* March 1982, 19:7, p.910.
368. Jean Aitchison. *British Book News* January 1982, p.33.
369. Aaron V. Cicourel. *Language in Society* 1983, 12:3, pp.356-358.
370. W. Keith Percival. [Unpublished review commissioned by *Language* and written in 1984 but never submitted]. Available at: http://people.ku.edu/~percival/RoyHarris4.html
371. Brian McHale. *Poetics Today* 1988, 9:4, pp.887-888.

APPROACHES TO LANGUAGE (1983)

372. [unsigned] CHOICE: *Current Reviews for Academic Libraries* September 1983, 21:1, p.90.

373. D.J. Allerton. *Linguistics* 1984, 22:5(273), pp.737-744.
374. Paul O. Takahara. *Language Sciences* 1985, 7:1, pp.231-239.

FERDINAND DE SAUSSURE. COURSE IN GENERAL LINGUISTICS Translated by Roy Harris (1983)

375. Paul Caron. "System of signs". *Times Educational Supplement* 15 July 1983, nr. 3498, p.21.
376. John Sturrock. "Where structuralism comes from". *London Review of Books* 2-15 February 1984, 6:2, pp.14-15.
377. Carol Sanders. "Saussure translated". *Historiographia Linguistica* 2000, 27:2-3, pp.345-358.
378. John E. Joseph. "Harris's Saussure—Harris as Saussure: the translations of the *Cours* and the *Third Course*". *Language Sciences* July 2011 33:4, pp.524-530.

DEVELOPMENTAL MECHANISMS OF LANGUAGE (1985)

379. Alan S. Kaye. *Language sciences* 1989, 11:1, pp.105-118.

THE ORIGIN OF WRITING (1986)

380. J.M.Y. Simpson. *British Book News* November 1986, p.643.
381. Roger T. Bell. "Picture-making". *Books & Bookmen* September 1986, p. 17.
382. John Weightman. "Not as simple as ABC: John Weightman on the history of writing". *Times Educational Supplement* 29 August 1986, nr. 3661, p.18.
383. John Chadwick. "Doing it by hand". *TLS. Times Literary Supplement* 29 August 1986, p.949.

384. Anthony Burgess. "Spelling it out". *The Observer* (London, England). 20 July 1986, p.22.
385. Marcel Danesi. *New Vico Studies* 1987, 5, pp.203-205.
386. Alexander George. *Language* March 1987, 63:1, pp.130-132.
387. Saul Levin. *General Linguistics* 1987, 27, p. 113-118.
388. Denise Schmandt-Besserat. *Libraries & Culture* Winter 1988, 23:1, pp.81-83.
389. W.C. Watt. "Getting writing right". *Semiotica* 1989, 75:3-4, pp.279-315.

THE LANGUAGE MACHINE (1987)

390. B.L. Dubois. ***CHOICE: Current Reviews for Academic Libraries*** June 1988, 25:10, pp.1549-1550.
391. Saul Levin. *General Linguistics* 1988, 28:3, pp.220-222.
392. Brian McHale. *Poetics Today* 1988, 9:4, pp.887-888.
393. Michael Toolan. *Language in Society* June 1989, 18:2, pp.269-275.
394. Robert D. Borsley. *Lingua* April 1990, 80:4, pp.359-362.

READING SAUSSURE: A CRITICAL COMMENTARY ON THE 'COURS DE LINGUISTIQUE GENERALE' (1987)

395. Brian McHale. *Poetics Today* 1988, 9:4, pp.887-888.
396. R.C. O'Hara. ***CHOICE: Current Reviews for Academic Libraries*** June 1988, 25:10, p.1550.
397. Katie Wales. *The Modern Language Review* January 1991, 86:1, pp.142-144.

LANGUAGE, SAUSSURE AND WITTGENSTEIN: HOW TO PLAY GAMES WITH WORDS (1988)

398. W. Taschek. *CHOICE: Current Reviews for Academic Libraries* January 1989, 26:5, p.819.
399. Peter Lamarque. "Shaky starts and flawed analogies". *TLS. Times Literary Supplement* 24 February 1989, nr. 4482, p.202.
400. Nigel Love. "Transcending Saussure". *Poetics Today* Winter 1989, 10:4, pp.793-818. [Review of Harris's books from 1980 through *Language, Saussure and Wittgenstein*.]
401. William Bennett. *The Modern Language Review* July 1990, 85:3, pp.740-741.
402. Rom Harré. *International Studies in Philosophy* 1991, 23:1, pp.118-119.
403. Ranjit Chatterjee. "To recognize the sign in the sign". *Semiotica* 1991 86:1-2 pp.109-114.
404. Ian Robinson. *Philosophical investigations* January 1992, 15:1 pp.83-89.
405. Paul O'Grady. *International Journal of Philosophical Studies* March 1993, 1:1, pp.148-150.
406. William Washabaugh. *Multilingua* 1994, 13:1-2, p.225.
407. Minna Vihla. *Neuphilologische Mitteilungen* 1997, 98:4, pp.433-435.

LINGUISTIC THOUGHT IN ENGLAND 1914–1945 (1988)

408. Peter Lamarque. "Shaky starts and flawed analogies". *TLS. Times Literary Supplement* 24 February 1989, nr. 4482, p.202..
409. Ladislav Zgusta. *Language* June 1990, 66:2, pp.416-417.
410. John Lyons. *Albion* Spring 1991, 23:1, pp.165-168.

LANDMARKS IN LINGUISTIC THOUGHT: THE WESTERN TRADITION FROM SOCRATES TO SAUSSURE (1989)

411. M.D. Linn. *CHOICE: Current Reviews for Academic Libraries* October 1989, 27:2, p.307.
412. Winfred P. Lehmann. *Language* September 1990, 66:3, pp.581-584.
413. Terrence Moore. *History of the Human Sciences* 1990, 3:2, pp.290-294.
414. Peter H. Salus. "Excerpts". *Semiotica* 1991, 86:1-2, pp.179-182.
415. J.D. Burnley. *The Review of English Studies* February 1992, 43:169, pp.90-91.
416. R.H. Robins. *Linguistics : an interdisciplinary journal of the language sciences* 1992, 30:3(319), pp.653-655.

THE FOUNDATIONS OF LINGUISTIC THEORY: SELECTED WRITINGS OF ROY HARRIS (1990)

417. Robert D. Borsley. *Journal of Linguistics* 1991, 27:1, pp.289-291.
418. Donald E. Hardy. *Language* September 1991, 67:3, pp.655-656.

SAUSSURE'S THIRD COURSE OF LECTURES ON GENERAL LINGUISTICS (1910–1911) : FROM THE NOTEBOOKS OF ÉMILE CONSTANTIN (1993)

419. Karen S. Chung. *Historiographia linguistica* 1994, 21:3, pp.448-451.
420. André Martinet. *La linguistique* 1995, 31:1, pp.143-144.
421. Yishai Tobin. "Will the real Professor de Saussure sign in, please? The three faces of Ferdinand". *Semiotica* 112:3-4, pp.391-402.

LINGUISTICS AND PHILOSOPHY: THE CONTROVERSIAL INTERFACE (1993)

422. Laurence Goldstein. *Language sciences* 1994, 16:3-4, pp.431-439.

LA SÉMIOLOGIE DE L'ÉCRITURE (1994)

423. Ghislaine Haas. *Linx* 1994, 31, pp.173-178.
424. Marie-Laure Raynaud. "Livres pratiques". *Réseaux* 1994, 12:67, pp.217-222.
425. Trudel Meisenburg. *Germanistik. Internationales Referatenorgan mit bibliographischen Hinweisen* 1995, 36:2, pp.370-371.

SIGNS OF WRITING (1995)

426. John Chadwick. "Sign o' the times". *Times Higher Education Supplement* 12 April 1996, nr. 1223, p.22.
427. Bernard Cerquiglini. *Histoire Épistémologie Langage* 1997, 19:1, pp.191-193.
428. J.L. Lemke. *Functions of Language* 1997, 4:1 pp.125-129.
429. Rebecca Hughes, Kieron O'Hara. *Language and Literature* 1997, 6:2, pp.151-156.
430. John Pier. *Style* Spring 1997, 31:1, pp.134-147.
431. J. Marshall Unger. *Modern Language Journal* Spring 1998, 82:1, p.123.
432. Crosley Shelvador. *Language* March 1998, 74:1, pp.209-210.
433. Tony Bex. *Journal of Literary Semantics* 1998 27:1 pp.58-60.
434. Karl Horst Schmidt. *Zeitschrift für Dialektologie und Linguistik* 1998, 65:1, pp.65-66.

435. J.S. Pettersson. "Delimiting a theory of writing", *Language Sciences* 1998, 20:4, pp.415-427.
436. Peter Gilderdale. *South African Journal of Psychology* June 1999, v. 29, nr. 2, p. 100–101.
437. Alan S. Kaye. *Word : Journal of the International Linguistic Association* April 1999, 50:1, pp.92-95.
438. Harald Haarmann. "Constructing culture: the realm of sign systems and beyond". *Semiotica* 2000, 132:3-4, pp.343-371.

THE ORIGIN OF LANGUAGE (1996)

439. David Crystal. "Necessary coupling". *Times Higher Education Supplement* 6 June 1997, nr. 1283, p.22.

THE LANGUAGE CONNECTION: PHILOSOPHY AND LINGUISTICS (1996)

440. David Crystal. "Necessary coupling". *Times Higher Education Supplement* 6 June 1997, nr. 1283, p.22-23.
441. Ross Cogan. *Cogito* 1997, 11:2, pp.133-135.
442. Siobhan Chapman. *Journal of Linguistics* September 1998, 34:2, pp.520-524.
443. Chris Bulcaen. *Pragmatics: quarterly publication of the International Pragmatics Association* 1998, 8:1, pp.104-105.
444. Richard McDonough. "Reflections on reflexivity". *Language Sciences* 2000, 22:2, pp.203-222.

SIGNS, LANGUAGE, AND COMMUNICATION: INTEGRATIONAL AND SEGREGATIONAL APPROACHES (1996)

445. Adrian Page. "Semiotics". *The Years Work in Critical and Cultural Theory* 1997, 7:1, pp.12-17.

446. J. Marshall Unger. *Modern Language Journal* Summer 1998, 82:2, pp.289-290.
447. Siobhan Chapman. *Journal of Linguistics* September 1998, 34:2, pp.520-524.
448. Alain Lemaréchal. *Bulletin de la Société de Linguistique de Paris* 1998, 93:2, pp.52-53.
449. Andrew Harrison. "Unscrambling chicken and egg". *Times Higher Education Supplement* 5 March 1999, nr. 1374, pp.30-31.
450. Hayley Davis. *Language and Literature* June 1999, 8:2, pp.183-185.
451. Boyd Davis. *Language* June 1999, 75:2, pp.383-384.
452. Karl Horst Schmidt. *Zeitschrift für Dialektologie und Linguistik* 1999, 66:2, pp.198-200.
453. David W. Samuels. *Anthropological Linguistics* Fall 1999, 41:3, pp.406-409.

LINGUISTICS INSIDE OUT: ROY HARRIS AND HIS CRITICS (1997)

454. Stephen Farrow. "Blast Roy Harris! The Great English Vortex". *Journal of Literary Semantics* 1998, 27:3, pp.190-197.
455. Alan S. Kaye. *Word* 2000, 51:3, pp.425-429.

INTRODUCTION TO INTEGRATIONAL LINGUISTICS (1998)

456. Chris Bulcaen. *Functions of language* 1998, 5:1, pp.103-106.
457. Jürgen Jaspers. *Pragmatics: quarterly publication of the International Pragmatics Association* September 1999, 9:3, pp.441-442.
458. Tony Bex. *Language and Literature* 2000, 9:4, pp.369-371.

459. Michael Toolan. *Language Awareness* 2000, 9:3, pp.160-162.
460. John Joseph. "Orthodox unorthodoxy". *Language Sciences* 2003, 25:1, pp.99-109.

INTEGRATIONAL LINGUISTICS: A FIRST READER (1998)

461. Tony Bex. *Language and Literature* 2000, 9:4, pp.369-371.

SIGNOS DE ESCRITURA (1999)

462. Jesús Camarero. "Una teoría de la escritura integracionista y semiológica". *Anthropos* (Barcelona) 2001, 192/193, pp.134-135.

RETHINKING WRITING (2000)

463. C. P. Jamison. *CHOICE: Current Reviews for Academic Libraries*. July–August 2001, 38:11-12, p.1952.
464. John Sturrock. "The everyday life of the alphabet". *TLS. Times Literary Supplement* 9 March 2001, nr. 5110, p.12.
465. Maria Ionita. "Quiet, Please!" *Literary Research/ Recherche litteraire* 2001, 18:35, pp.192-197.
466. Florian Coulmas. *Written Language & Literacy* 2001, 4:2, pp.215-218.
467. [unsigned] *European Journal of Communication* December 2001, 16:4, p.563.
468. W.C. Watt. "Mere writing". *Semiotica* 2002, 141:1-4, pp.453-476.
469. Geoffrey Sampson. "Dead Swiss in rash comments shock. ('*Rethinking Writing*')". *Times Higher Education Supplement* 15 February 2002, nr.1525, p.28.

470. Matthew Bullen. *Rocky Mountain Review* Spring 2003, 57:1, pp.121-122.
471. David R. Olson. *Language in Society* February 2004, 33:3, pp.449-452.
472. Naomi S. Baron. "Rethinking written culture". *Language Sciences* 2004, 26:1, pp.57-96.
473. Fiona Glade. *Discourse Studies* May 2004, v. 6, nr. 2, p. 280–282.
474. Stephen Pierson. *International Journal of Applied Semiotics* 2005, 4:2, pp.131-132.

SAUSSURE AND HIS INTERPRETERS (2001)

475. Jacques Guy. "Gurus not Saussure about their idol's work". *Times Higher Education Supplement* 29 June 2001, nr.1493, p.27.
476. Craig A. Hamilton. "How to do things with Saussure: *Saussure and His Interpreters*". *Language and Literature* 2002, 11:3, pp.264-267.
477. David Herman. "Saussure and the grounds of intepretation". *Postmodern Culture* 2002, 13:1.
478. Stephen Farrow. *The Use of English* Autumn 2003, 55:1, pp.86-89.
479. Carol Sanders. *The Modern Language Review* October 2004, 99:4, pp.1064-1065.
480. Hilla Karas. *Lingvisticae Investigationes* 2006, 29:2, pp.313-317.

THE LANGUAGE MYTH IN WESTERN CULTURE (2002)

481. Alan S. Kaye. *Language* September 2003, 79:3, pp.655-656.
482. Peter Muhlhäusler. *Language in Society* April 2004, 33:2, pp.285-289.

SAUSSURE AND HIS INTERPRETERS (2nd, ed. 2003)

483. Denis Bouchard. "Le Maître de Genèveu". *The Canadian Journal of Linguistics/La revue canadienne de linguistique* June 2004, 49:2, pp.223-241.
484. Jonathan D. Culler. *Language* December 2006, 82:4, pp.915-918.

HISTORY, SCIENCE, AND THE LIMITS OF LANGUAGE: AN INTEGRATIONIST APPROACH (2003)

485. Andreea Calude. "The science of numbers: does language help or hinder?" *Language Sciences* July 2011 33:4, pp.562-568.

LA TIRANNIA DELL'ALFABETO (2003)

486. Marc Wilhelm Küster. Semiotik der Schrift. In his: *Geordnetes Weltbild: die Tradition des alphabetischen Sortierens von der Keilschrift bis zur EDV: eine Kulturgeschichte.* Tübingen: Niemeyer Verlag, 2006. p. 32-39.

THE NECESSITY OF ARTSPEAK (2003)

487. Leonard R.N. Ashley. *Geolinguistics* 2003, 29, p.101.
488. Laura Gascoigne. "Tell me, Professor: Where's the art in that?" *The Jackdaw* October 2003.

THE LINGUISTICS OF HISTORY (2004)

489. Michael Bentley. "Open the shops". *TLS. Times Literary Supplement* 1 April 2005, nr. 5322, p.31.

490. C. Behan McCullagh. "Language and the truth of history". *History and Theory* October 2005, 44, pp.441-455.
491. Peter Burke. *American Historical Review* June 2006, 111:3, pp.784-785.
492. Stephen Farrow. *The Use of English* 2006, 58:1, pp.78-81.
493. Don E. Walicek. *Journal of English Linguistics* 2007, 35, pp.196-201.
494. Andreea Calude. *eLanguage* Posted February 16th, 2010 http://elanguage.net/blogs/booknotices/?p=248.

THE SEMANTICS OF SCIENCE (2005)

495. Madalena Cruz-Ferreira. *The Linguist list* 16.3004, Mon 17 October 2005. http://linguistlist.org/issues/16/16-3004.html.
496. David Bade. *Journal of Documentation* 2006, 62:1, pp.145-153.
497. Jan Wawrzyńak. *Pantaneto Forum* October 2006, nr.24. http://www.pantaneto.co.uk/issue24/wawrzyniak.htm.
498. Randy Harris. *Language in Society* November 2007, 36:5, pp.802-805.
499. David Spurrett. "How to semanticize science and sell it short". *Language Sciences* January 2009, 31:1, pp.97-110.
500. Rom Harré. "Integrating surrogationalism". *Language Sciences* July 2011, 33:4, pp.569-574.

INTEGRATIONIST NOTES AND PAPERS, 2003–2005 (2006)

501. Paul Cobley. "The little book of academic truth and freedom". *Language & Communication* October 2007, 27:4, pp.433-435.

DEFINITION IN THEORY AND PRACTICE: LANGUAGE, LEXICOGRAPHY AND THE LAW (2007)

502. David Bade. *Journal of Documentation* 2007, 63:6, pp.987-992.
503. Stuart Hannabuss. *Library Review* May 2009, 58:5, pp.396-397.
504. Chris Heffer. *Journal of Sociolinguistics* 2009, 13:3, pp.419-423.
505. Michael Toolan. "Legal definitions". *Language & Communication* April 2009, 29:2, pp.182-192.
506. Natalia D. Jacobsen. *Applied Linguistics* 2010, 31:5, pp.734-737.

MINDBOGGLING: PRELIMINARIES TO A SCIENCE OF THE MIND (2008)

507. Richard L. Gregory. "Synapses, signs and language". *Times Higher Education* 13 November 2008, nr.1871, p.54.
508. David Bade. *Journal of Documentation* 2009, 65:6, pp.1027-1036.
509. Wes Sharrock and Jeff Coulter. "After interpretation: Roy Harris on mind and knowledge". *Language Sciences* July 2011, 33:4, pp.519-523.

RATIONALITY AND THE LITERATE MIND (2009)

510. Raphael Salkie. "Strange death of Oxford linguistics". *Times Higher Education* 27 August 2009, nr.1911, p.48.
511. David Bade. *Journal of Documentation* 2009, 65:6, pp.1027-1036.
512. Dennis Ryan. *eLanguage* 13 December 2010. http://elanguage.net/blogs/booknotices/?p=1266.

513. Vladimir Žegarac. *Writing & Pedagogy* 2011, 3:1, pp.169-174.

AFTER EPISTEMOLOGY (2009)

514. David Bade. *Journal of Documentation* 2011, 67:1, pp.194-200.
515. Wes Sharrock and Jeff Coulter. "After interpretation: Roy Harris on mind and knowledge". *Language Sciences* July 2011, 33:4, pp.519-523.

THE GREAT DEBATE ABOUT ART (2010)

516. John Rapko. "The Arts Died with Dada: Roy Harris and the Great Debate About Art". *Artcritical: the online magazine of art and ideas* Tuesday, August 17th, 2010. http://artcritical.com/2010/08/17/the-arts-died-with-dada-roy-harris-and-the-great-debate-about-art/.

III. Integrational Linguistics and Related Works

A. Bibliography.

517. "Roy Harris: a chronological bibliography". *The Foundations of Linguistic Theory. Selected Writings of Roy Harris*. Edited by Nigel Love. London: Routledge, 1990. pp.ix-xv.
518. "Roy Harris: Publications 1956-1995". *Linguistics Inside Out: Roy Harris and his Critics*. Edited by George Wolf and Nigel Love. Amsterdam/Philadelphia: John Benjamins, 1997. pp.xv-xxvii.
519. "Roy Harris bibliography 1996-2010" ***Language Sciences*** July 2011, 33:4, pp.480-485.
520. David Bade. "Roy Harris in review 1973-2011". ***Language Sciences*** July 2011, 33:4, pp.486-497.
521. Integrationists' repository. www.integrationistsrepository.com

B. Collections

522. David Bade and Adrian Pablé (eds.). *Linguistics Out of Bounds : Explorations in Integrational Linguistics in Honour of Roy Harris on His 80th Birthday*. Amsterdam: Elsevier, 2011. Special issue of ***Language Sciences*** July 2011, v.33:4, pp.475-724.
523. Hayley G. Davis and Talbot J. Taylor (eds.). *Redefining Linguistics*. London and New York: Routledge, 1990. vii + 172 pp.
524. Hayley G. Davis and Talbot J. Taylor (eds.). *Rethinking Linguistics*. London and New York: Routledge, 2003. (Communication and Linguistic Theory Series) ix + 191 pp.
525. Roy Harris (ed.). *The Language Myth in Western Culture*. London: Curzon, 2002. (Communication and Linguistic Theory) vii + 228 pp.

526. Roy Harris and George Wolf (eds.). *Integrational Linguistics: a First Reader*. Oxford: Pergamon, 1998. (Language & Communication Library, v. 18) vii + 350 pp.
527. John E. Joseph and Talbot J. Taylor (eds.). *Ideologies of Language*. London and New York: Routledge, 1990. (Routledge Politics of Language Series)
528. Nigel Love (ed.). *Language and History: Integrationist Perspectives*. London and New York: Routledge, 2006. (Routledge Advances in Communication and Linguistic Theory, 4) viii+ 242 pp.
529. David Spurrett (ed.). *Distributed Cognition and Integrational Linguistics*. Special issue of **Language Sciences** 2004, 26:6, pp.497-742.
530. Talbot J. Taylor (ed.). *The Philosophy of Linguistics: Essays in Honor of Roy Harris*. Special issue of **Language Sciences** 1997, 19:1, pp.1-100.
531. Michael J. Toolan (ed.). *Language Teaching: Integrational Linguistics Approaches*. New York & London: Routledge, 2009. (Routledge advances in communication and linguistic theory, 6) viii + 182 pp.
532. George Wolf (ed.). *New Departures in Linguistics*. New York: Garland, 1992. (Garland Reference Library of the Humanities, vol. 1406) ix + 265 pp.
533. George Wolf and Nigel Love (eds.). *Linguistics Inside Out: Roy Harris and His Critics*. Amsterdam-Philadelphia: John Benjamins, 1997. (Amsterdam Studies in the Theory and History of Linguistic Science, vol. 148) xxvii + 344 pp.

C.   Philosophy. Methodology. Semiology

For publications by Roy Harris, see Part I; for reviews of those publications, see Part II.

534. Salvatore Attardo. Review of Talbot J. Taylor. *Mutual Misunderstanding: Scepticism and the Theorizing of*

Language and Interpretation. ***Discourse and Society*** 1995, 6:2, pp.297-298.
535. Sylvain Auroux. "Le mode d'existence de la « langue »". ***La linguistique*** 2013, 49:1, pp.11-33.
536. David Bade. "Signs unsigned and meanings not meant: linguistic theory and hypothetical, simulated, imitation, and meaningless language". ***Language Sciences*** 2012, 34:3, pp.361–375.
537. David Bade. "Respondeo etsi mutabor: Eugen Rosenstock-Huessy and Linguistic Theory". Darrol Bryant (ed.), *Eugen Rosenstock-Huessy, Then and Now*. Waterloo, Ontario, Canada: Eugen Rosenstock-Huessy Society, 2014, pp. 20-50.
538. David Bade. "Respondeo etsi mutabor: Eugen Rosenstock-Huessy's semiological Zweistromland". ***Culture, Theory and Critique***, 2015, 56:1, pp.87-100 (abridgement of the preceding)
539. David Bade and Adrian Pablé. "Signs unfounded and confounded: a reply to Søren Lund". ***RASK, International tidsskrift for sprog og kommunikation*** 2012, 35, pp.43-85.
540. Katharina Barbe. "The dilemma with dichotomies". ***Language & Communication*** 2001, 21:1, pp.89-103.
541. Naomi S. Baron. "Contextualizing "context": from Malinowski to machine translation". George Wolf and Nigel Love (eds.), *Linguistics Inside Out*. Amsterdam: John Benjamins, 1997. pp.151-181.
542. Louis S. Berger. *Language and the Ineffable: A Developmental Perspective and Its Applications*. Plymouth, UK: Lexington Books, 2011. 147 pp.
543. Robert D. Borsley. Review of Hayley G. Davis and Talbot J. Taylor (eds.), *Redefining Linguistics*. Routledge, London and New York, 1990. ***Lingua*** 1992, 88:1, pp.67-71.
544. Robert D. Borsley and Frederick J. Newmeyer. "The language muddle: Roy Harris and generative grammar".

George Wolf and Nigel Love (eds.), *Linguistics Inside Out.* Amsterdam: John Benjamins, 1997. pp.42-64.
545. Jesús Camarero. "Integrational semiology and epistemo-criticism". *Language Sciences* July 2011, 33:4, pp.662-666.
546. Deborah Cameron, Elizabeth Frazer, Penelope Harvey, M. B. H. Rampton, and Kay Richardson. *Researching Language: Issues of Power and Method.* London & New York: Routledge. 1992. (The Politics of Language Series) 148pp.
547. Philip Carr. "Facthood and reality in linguistics: A reply to Love". *Language & Communication* 1994, 14:4, pp. 391-402.
548. Philip Carr. "Telementation and generative linguistics". George Wolf and Nigel Love (eds.), *Linguistics Inside Out.* Amsterdam: John Benjamins, 1997. pp.65-83.
549. Philip Carr. "The mythical, the non-mythical and representation in linguistics". Roy Harris (ed.). *The Language Myth in Western Culture.* London: Curzon, 2002. pp.84-99.
550. Philipp Carr. "Internalism, externalism and coding". *Language Sciences* 2007, 29:5, pp.672-689.
551. Philip Carr. "The philosophy of phonology". *Philosophy of Linguistics* 2012, pp.403-444.
552. Siobhan Chapman. "In defence of a code: linguistic meaning and propositionality in verbal communication." *Journal of Pragmatics* 2001, 33:10, pp.1553-1570.
553. Noël Christe and Jérémie Wenger. "La fin justifie-t-elle les moyens? A derridean halt in Harris' long walk". *Language Sciences* July 2011, 33:4, pp.531-532.
554. Paul Cobley. "Mythbusting". *Language Sciences* July 2011, 33:4, pp.511-516.
555. Stephen J. Cowley. "Conversational functions of rhythmical patterning: a behavioural perspective". *Language & Communication* 1994, 14:4, 353-376.
556. Tony Crowley. "That obscure object of desire: a science of language". John E. Joseph and Talbot J. Taylor (eds.).

Ideologies of Language. London and New York: Routledge, 1990. pp.27-50.
557. Bjarke Damm. "Hvad er sprog i virkeligheden? Strukturalisme eller integrationisme?". ***Nydanske sprogstudier*** 2007, 36, pp.151-172.
558. Daniel R. Davis. "The three-dimensional sign". ***Language Sciences*** 1997, 19:1, pp.23-31.
559. Daniel R. Davis. "Wittgenstein, integrational linguistics, and the myth of normativity". ***Language & Communication*** 1999, 19:1, pp.69-95.
560. Hayley G. Davis. "Introduction". Hayley G. Davis and Talbot J. Taylor (eds.), *Redefining Linguistics*. London and New York: Routledge, 1990. pp.1-17.
561. Hayley G. Davis. "Drawing the morphological line". George Wolf (ed.). *New Departures in Linguistics*. New York: Garland, 1992. pp.90-115.
562. Hayley G. Davis. "The interdependence of lexicography and linguistic theory". ***Journal of Literary Semantics*** 1994, 23, pp.188-199.
563. Hayley G. Davis. "Ordinary people's philosophy: Comparing lay and professional metalinguistic knowledge". ***Language Sciences*** 1997, 19:1, pp.33-46.
564. Hayley G. Davis. *Words: an Integrational Approach*. London: Curzon, 2001. (Communication and Linguistic Theory) xi + 218 pp.
565. Hayley G. Davis. "The linguistic individual: an integrational approach". ***Language Sciences*** 2001, 23:6, pp.707-713.
566. Hayley G. Davis. "Introduction: why rethink linguistics?" Hayley G. Davis and Talbot J. Taylor (eds.). *Rethinking Linguistics*. London and New York: Routledge, 2003. pp.1-16.
567. Dorthe Duncker. "On the empirical challenge to integrational studies in language". ***Language Sciences*** July 2011, 33:4, pp.533-542.

568. Dorthe Duncker. "Norm, situering og sproglige kendsgerninger". *Danske Talesprog* 2012, 11, pp.3-44.
569. Dorthe Duncker. "'What's it called?': Conventionalization, glossing practices, and linguistic (in)determinacy". *Language & Communication* 2012, 32:4, pp.400-419.
570. Steve Farrow. "The nature of syntax and the syntax of nature". *Language & Communication* 1994, 14:2, pp.203-210.
571. Steve Farrow. "Irony and theories of meaning". George Wolf (ed.). *New Departures in Linguistics*. New York: Garland, 1992. pp.135-145. Reprinted in Roy Harris and George Wolf (eds.). *Integrational Linguistics: a First Reader*. Oxford: Pergamon, 1998. pp.159-167.
572. Steve Farrow. "The language myth revisited". *Language & Communication* 2005, 25:1, pp.19-25.
573. David Fleming. "The search for an integrational account of language: Roy Harris and conversation analysis". *Language Sciences* 1995, 17:1, pp.73-98.
574. David Fleming. "Is ethnomethodological conversation analysis an "integrational" account of language?". George Wolf and Nigel Love (eds.), *Linguistics Inside Out*. Amsterdam: John Benjamins, 1997. pp.182-207.
575. Cécile Gretsch. "Pragmatics and integrational linguistics". *Language & Communication* 2009, 29:4, pp.328-342.
576. Marc Haas and Roy Harris. "'The question is not whether integrationism can survive outside linguistics, but whether linguistics can survive outside integrationism': an Interview with Roy Harris". *Language Sciences* July 2011, 33:4, pp.498-502.
577. Rom Harré. "Rules and algorithms: Wittgenstein on language". George Wolf and Nigel Love (eds.), *Linguistics Inside Out*. Amsterdam: John Benjamins, 1997. pp.136-150.
578. Jesper Hermann. "Visse vrangforestillinger om ordet "sprog" – eller hvordan vor brug af ordet "sprog"

forhindrer vi forstår". Peter Widell & Ulf Dalvad Berthelsen (eds.) *11. Møde om Udforskningen af Dansk Sprog, Nordisk Institut, Aarhus Universitet 12.-13. oktober 2006*. Århus: Nordisk Institut, Aarhus Universitet, 2007. pp.118-130.
579. Jesper Hermann. "Ordet 'sprog' som lingvistikkens flogiston". Henrik Jørgensen and Peter Widell (eds.), *Det bedre argument: festskrift til Ole Togeby 7. marts 2007*. Århus: Wessel og Huitfeldt, 2007. pp.233-244.
580. John Hewson. Review of Hayley Davis and Talbot Taylor (eds.), *Redefining Linguistics*, **Canadian Journal of Linguistics** 1992, 37, pp.378-381.
581. Paul Hopper. "The emergence of the category 'proper name' in discourse". Hayley Davis and Talbot Taylor (eds.), *Redefining Linguistics*. London and New York: Routledge, 1990. pp.149-162.
582. Werner Hüllen. Review of Talbot J. Taylor. *Mutual Misunderstanding: Scepticism and the Theorizing of Language and Interpretation*. **Historiographia Linguistica** 1994, 21:1/2. pp.227-231.
583. Christopher M. Hutton. "Meaning and the principle of linearity". **Language & Communication** 1990, 10:3, pp.169-183. Reprinted in Roy Harris and George Wolf (eds.). *Integrational Linguistics: a First Reader*. Oxford: Pergamon, 1998. pp.126-142.
584. Christopher M. Hutton. *Abstraction & Instance; the Type-Token Relation in Linguistic Theory*. Oxford: Pergamon Press, 1990. (Language & Communication Library, v. 11) viii + 180 pp.
585. Christopher Hutton. "Arbitrariness and rational signs". George Wolf (ed.). *New Departures in Linguistics*. New York: Garland, 1992. pp.250-259.
586. Christopher M. Hutton. Review of Talbot J. Taylor. *Mutual Misunderstanding: Scepticism and the Theorizing*

of Language and Interpretation. **Language Sciences** 1993, 15:3, pp. 261-267.
587. Christopher M. Hutton. "The 'dictator of taste': Rules, regularities and responsibilities". **Language Sciences** 1997, 19:1, pp.47-55
588. Christopher M. Hutton. "Semantics and the 'etymological fallacy' fallacy". **Language Sciences** 1998, 20:2, pp.189-200.
589. Christopher M. Hutton. "Universalism and human difference in Chomskyan linguistics: the first 'superhominid' and the language faculty". D.A. Kibbee (ed.), *Chomskyan (R)evolutions*. Amsterdam: John Benjamins Publishing Company, 2010. pp.337-352.
590. Christopher Hutton. "The politics of the language myth: reflections on the writings of Roy Harris". **Language Sciences** July 2011, 33:4, pp.503-510.
591. Christopher M. Hutton and Adrian Pablé. "Semiotic profile: Roy Harris". **SemiotiX** 2011 http://semioticon.com/semiotix/2011/01/semiotic-profile-roy-harris/
592. Christopher Hutton, Adrian Pablé, David Bade. "Roy Harris and Integrational Linguistics". **Language Sciences** July 2011, 33:4, pp.475-479.
593. Peter Jones. "Reality check: Some thoughts in response to Pablé". *Social Epistemology Review and Reply Collective* 10 October 2013, 2:11, pp.16-19. http://social-epistemology.com/2013/10/10/reality-check-some-thoughts-in-response-to-pable-peter-e-jones/
594. John E. Joseph. "The end of languages as we know them". *Anglistik* 1997, 8:2, pp.31-46.
595. John E. Joseph. "The 'Language Myth' myth: Roy Harris's red herrings". George Wolf and Nigel Love (eds.), *Linguistics Inside Out*. Amsterdam: John Benjamins, 1997. pp.9-41.

596. John E. Joseph. "Rethinking linguistic creativity". Hayley G. Davis and Talbot J. Taylor (eds.). *Rethinking Linguistics.* London and New York: Routledge, 2003. pp.121-150.
597. John E. Joseph and Talbot J. Taylor. "Ideology, science and language". John E. Joseph and Talbot J. Taylor (eds.). *Ideologies of Language.* London and New York: Routledge, 1990. pp.1-8.
598. Diana Kilpert. "Getting the full picture: a reflection on the work of M.A.K. Halliday". **Language Sciences** 2003, 25:2, pp.159-209.
599. Kravchenko, Alexander V. "Essential properties of language, or, why language is not a code". **Language Sciences** 2007, 29:5, pp.650-671.
600. Alexander V. Kravchenko. "Reassessing the project of linguistics". Jordan Zlatev, Mats Andrén, Marlene J. Falck, and Carita Lundmark (eds.), *Studies in Language and Cognition.* Newcastle upon Tyne: Cambridge Scholars Publishing, 2009. pp.27-42.
601. Alexander V. Kravchenko. "Native speakers, mother tongues, and other objects of wonder". **Language Sciences** 2010, 32:6, pp.677-785.
602. Ron Kuzar. "Split word, split subject, split society". ***Pragmatics*** 1997, 7:1, pp.21-54.
603. D. Lee. Review of George Wolf (ed.), *New Departures in Linguistics.* **Journal of Literary Semantics** 1993, 22:2, pp.165-175.
604. Ruiqing Liang. "Digitality, granularity and ineffability". **Language Sciences** 2011, 33:1, pp.30-39.
605. Nigel Love. "Making sense of Chomsky's revolution". **Language & Communication** 1981, 1:2-3, pp.275-287.
606. Nigel Love. "Psychologistic structuralism and the polylect". **Language & Communication** 1984, 4:3, pp.225-240.

607. Nigel Love. "The fixed-code theory". *Language & Communication* 1985, 5:1 p.1-17. Reprinted in Roy Harris and George Wolf (eds.). *Integrational Linguistics: a First Reader*. Oxford: Pergamon, 1998. pp.49-67.
608. Nigel Love. "Ideal linguistics". *Language & Communication* 1988, 8:1, pp.69-84.
609. Nigel Love. "Language and the science of the impossible: T. Pateman, *Language in Mind and Language in Society: Studies in Linguistic Reproduction*. Clarendon Press, Oxford, 1987". *Language & Communication* 1989, 9:4, pp.269-287.
610. Nigel Love. "The locus of languages in a redefined linguistics". Hayley G. Davis and Talbot J. Taylor (eds.), *Redefining Linguistics*. London and New York: Routledge, 1990. pp.53-117. Adaptation of pages 95-114 printed in Roy Harris and George Wolf (eds.). *Integrational Linguistics: a First Reader*. Oxford: Pergamon, 1998. pp.96-110.
611. Nigel Love. "Generativism, genes and grammar". *Language & Communication* 1991, 11:1-2, pp.71-73.
612. Nigel Love. "Linguistic realities". *Language & Communication* 1992, 12:1, pp.79-92.
613. Nigel Love. "On the need for a new departure in phonology". George Wolf (ed.). *New Departures in Linguistics*. New York: Garland, 1992. p.60-89.
614. Nigel Love. "Integrating Austin". *Language Sciences* 1997, 19:1, pp.57-65.
615. Nigel Love. "Searle on language". *Language & Communication* 1999, 19:1, pp.9-25.
616. Nigel Love. "Rethinking the fundamental assumption of linguistics". Hayley G. Davis and Talbot J. Taylor (eds.), *Rethinking Linguistics*. London and New York: Routledge, 2003. pp.69-94.
617. Nigel Love. "Are languages digital codes?" *Language Sciences* 2007, 29:5, pp.690-709.

618. Nigel Love. "Science, language and linguistic culture". *Language & Communication* 2009, 29:1, pp.26-46.
619. Søren Lund. "On Professor Roy Harris's 'Integrational Turn' in linguistics". *RASK, Internationalt tidsskrift for sprog og kommunikation* 2012, 35, pp.3-42.
620. Juan Carlos Moreno Cabrera. "Speech and gesture: an integrational approach". *Language Sciences* July 2011, 33:4, pp.615-622.
621. Juan Carlos Moreno Cabrera. *Cuestiones Clave de la Lingüística*. Madrid: Síntesis, 2012. 222pp.
622. Salikoko Mufwene. Review of George Wolf (ed.), *New Departures in Linguistics*. *Journal of Pidgin and Creole Languages* 1994, 9:2, pp.414-416.
623. Peter Mühlhäusler. "Comments on Newmeyer's 'functional explanation in linguistics and the origins of language'". *Language & Communication* 1991, 11:1-2, pp.75-78.
624. Brigitte Nerlich. "Saussurean linguistics and the problem of meaning: from dynamic statics to static dynamics". *Language & Communication* 1986, 6:4, pp.267-276.
625. Adrian Pablé. "Language, knowledge and reality: the integrationist on name variation". *Language & Communication* 2010, 30:2, pp.109-122.
626. Adrian Pablé. "Hvordan forholder integrationismen sig til den virkelige verden". *Spindet. Sprogpsykologisk Information og Debat* 2010, 10:2, pp.16-21. Translated from English into Danish by Bent Holshagen Hemmingsen.
627. Adrian Pablé. "Integrating the real". *Language Sciences* 2011, 33:1, pp.20-29.
628. Adrian Pablé. "Logophilia, logophobia and the *terra mota* of personal linguistic experience". *Language & Communication* 2012, 32:3, pp.257-264.
629. Adrian Pablé. "Towards a new semiotics of landmark knowledge". *Social Semiotics* 2012, 22:3, pp.259-274.

630. Adrian Pablé. "An integrational response to Searlean realism, or how language does not relate to consciousness". *Semiotica* 2013, 193:1, pp.101-118.
631. Adrian Pablé. "Reality re-checked and Galileo re-integrated: A reply to Jones and Spurrett." *Social Epistemology Review and Reply Collective (SERRC)* 2014, 3:2, pp.49-57.
632. Adrian Pablé. "Integrating Rorty and (social) constructivism. A view from Harrisian semiology". *Social Epistemology* 2015, 29:1, pp.95-117
633. Adrian Pablé and Chris Hutton. *Signs, Meaning and Experience.* Berlin: Mouton De Gruyter, 2015. (Semiotics, Communication and Cognition, 15) xvii + 180pp.
634. 彭新竹. Peng Xin-zhu. "从"概念整合理论"管窥学科整合趋势" "On disciplinary integration from the view of conceptual integration theory". 外语学刊 *Foreign Language Research* 2013, 5, pp.31-35.
635. Kanavillil Rajagopalan. "On Searle [on Austin] on language". *Language & Communication* 2000, 20:4, pp.347-391.
636. Liam Roger. "Is a bilingual dictionary possible?" Anna Braasch and Claus Povlsen (eds.), *Proceedings of the Tenth EURALEX International Congress, EURALEX 2002, Copenhagen, Denmark, August 13-17, 2002.* København: Center for Sprogteknologi, 2002. pp.435-440.
637. Stuart G. Shanker. Review of: Michael Toolan, *Total Speech. An Integrational Linguistic Approach to Language.* Durham and London: Duke University Press, 1996. *Metaphor and Symbol* 1998, 13, pp.235-241.
638. Wes Sharrock and Jeff Coulter. "After interpretation: Roy Harris on mind and knowledge". *Language Sciences* July 2011, 33:4, pp.519-523.
639. Maarja Siiner. "Sprogets refleksivitet: det er lige så svært at spørge om sprog som at tale om det". *Spindet* 2004, 4:4, pp.13-17.

640. Catherine Slater. "Generative phonology in the dock". *Language & Communication* 1982, 2:3, pp.311-319. (review of Nigel Love, *Generative phonology*.)
641. P. Stockwell. Review of Michael Toolan. *Total Speech: An Integrational Linguistic Approach to Language*. Durham and London: Duke University Press, 1996. *Language and Literature* 1999, 8:1, pp.78-81.
642. Andrei Stoevsky. "Towards an integrational approach in linguistics". Christopher S. Butler, Raquel Hidalgo Downing, Julia Lavid (eds.), *Functional Perspectives on Grammar and Discourse: In honour of Angela Downing*. Amsterdam: John Benjamins, 2007. (Studies in Language Companion Series, 85) pp.81-95.
643. Janusz Stopyra. "Einige Bemerkungen zum Integrationslinguistik von Roy Harris". *Orbis Linguarum* 2002, 22, pp.83-89.
644. Talbot J. Taylor. "A Wittgensteinian perspective in linguistics". *Language & Communication* 1981, 1:2-3, pp.263-274.
645. Talbot J. Taylor. "Editing rules and understanding: the case against sentence-based syntax". *Language & Communication* 1984, 4:2, pp.105-127. Reprinted as "Conversational utterances and sentences" in Roy Harris and George Wolf (eds.). *Integrational Linguistics: a First Reader*. Oxford: Pergamon, 1998. pp.171-187.
646. Talbot J. Taylor. "Do you understand? Criteria of understanding in verbal interaction". *Language & Communication* 1986, 6:3, pp.171-180. Reprinted in his *Theorizing Language* (Oxford: Pergamon, 1997), pp.79-92; also reprinted in G. MacGregor (ed.), *Language for Hearers*. Oxford: Pergamon Press, 1986; and in Roy Harris and George Wolf (eds.). *Integrational Linguistics: a First Reader*. Oxford: Pergamon, 1998. pp.198-208.
647. Talbot J. Taylor. "Linguistic agency and the normativity of language". *The Sixteenth Lacus Forum*. Lake Bluff, Ill.:

Linguistics Association of Canada and the United States, 1991. pp.122-130.

648. Talbot J. Taylor. "Normativity and linguistic form". Hayley G. Davis and Talbot J. Taylor (eds.). *Redefining Linguistics.* London and New York: Routledge, 1990. pp.118-148.

649. Talbot J. Taylor. "Which is to be master? The institutionalization of authority in the science of language". John E. Joseph and Talbot J. Taylor (eds.). *Ideologies of Language.* London/New York: Routledge, 1990. pp.9-26.

650. Talbot J. Taylor. "Communicational scepticism and the discourse of order". George Wolf (ed.). *New Departures in Linguistics.* New York: Garland, 1992. pp.163-179.

651. Talbot J. Taylor. *Mutual Misunderstanding: Scepticism and the Theorizing of Language and Interpretation.* Durham and London: Duke University Press, 1992. (Post-Contemporary Interventions) xii + 266 pp.

652. Talbot J. Taylor. "Why we need a theory of language". Rom Harré and Roy Harris (eds.). *Linguistics and Philosophy: The Controversial Interface.* Oxford: Pergamon, 1993. pp.233-248.

653. Talbot J. Taylor. *L'incomprensione linguistica - Lo scetticismo e la teorizazione del linguaggio e dell'interpretazione.* Rome: G. Laterza Publishing Co., 1996. (Italian translation of *Mutual Misunderstanding*).

654. Talbot J. Taylor. "Roy Harris and the philosophy of linguistics". **Language Sciences** 1997, 19:1, pp.1-5.

655. Talbot J. Taylor. *Theorizing Language: Analysis, Normativity, Rhetoric, History.* Amsterdam, New York and Oxford: Pergamon, 1997. x + 271 pp.

656. Talbot J. Taylor. "Language constructing language: the implications of reflexivity for linguistic theory". **Language Sciences** 2000, 22:4, pp.483-499.

657. Talbot J. Taylor. "Language constructing language: the implications of reflexivity for linguistic theory". Hayley G.

Davis and Talbot J. Taylor (eds.). *Rethinking Linguistics.* London and New York: Routledge, 2003. pp.95-120. (Revised version of the preceding entry)

658. Talbot J. Taylor and Deborah Cameron. *Analysing Conversation: Rules and Units in the Structure of Talk.* Oxford: Pergamon Press, 1987. (Language & Communication Library, v. 9) viii + 169 pp.

659. Talbot J. Taylor and George Wolf. "Performatives and the descriptivist's dilemmas". **Journal of Linguistics** 1981, 17:2, pp.329-332.

660. Wolfgang Teubert. *Meaning, Discourse and Society.* Cambridge: Cambridge University Press, 2010. viii + 290 pp.

661. Wolfgang Teubert. "Was there a cat in the garden? Knowledge between discourse and the monadic self". **Language and Dialogue** 3:2. 2013 pp.273-297.

662. Michael Toolan. "Largely for against theory". **Journal of Literary Semantics** 1990, 19:3, pp.150-166.

663. Michael Toolan. "Perspectives on literal meaning". **Language & Communication** 1991, 11:4, pp.333-351.

664. Michael Toolan. "On relevance-theory". George Wolf (ed.). *New Departures in Linguistics.* New York: Garland, 1992. pp.146-162.

665. Michael Toolan. *Total Speech: an Integrational Linguistic Approach to Language.* Durham and London: Duke University Press, 1996. (Post-Contemporary Interventions) 337 pp.

666. Michael Toolan. "A few words on telementation". **Language Sciences** 1997, 19:1, pp.79-91. Reprinted in Roy Harris and George Wolf (eds.). *Integrational Linguistics: a First Reader.* Oxford: Pergamon, 1998. pp.68-82.

667. Tanya de Villiers. "Why Peirce matters: the symbol in Deacon's *Symbolic Species*". **Language Sciences** 2007, 29:1, pp.88-108.

668. Jan K. Wawrzyniak. "Communicational scepticism and the linguist". *Language Sciences* 2006, 28:4, pp.436-445.
669. Jan K. Wawrzyniak. "Native speakers, mother tongues and natural semantic metalanguages." *Language Sciences* 2010, 32:6, pp.648-670.
670. Edda Weigand. "The language myth and linguistics humanised". Roy Harris (ed.). *The Language Myth in Western Culture*. London: Curzon, 2002. pp.55-83.
671. Edda Weigand. "Linguists and their speakers". *Language Sciences* 2003, 32:5, pp.536-544.
672. Edda Weigand. *Language as Dialogue: From Rules to Principles of Probability*. Amsterdam: John Benjamins, 2009. (Dialogue Studies, 5) viii + 410 pp.
673. Edda Weigand. "Paradigm changes in linguistics: from reductionism to holism". *Language Sciences* July 2011, 33:4. pp.544-550.
674. Jérémie Wenger and Noël Christe. "Of fig and foes". *Language Sciences* July 2011, 33:4, pp.517-518.
675. Chris Werry. *Rhetoric and Reflexivity in Chomskyan and Cognitive Linguistics*. Ph.D. dissertation in Rhetoric, Carnegie Mellon University, 2002.
676. Chris Werry. "Language as vision: the ocularcentrism of Chomskyan Linguistics". *LORE* 2002, 2:2. Available at http://www.lorejournal.org/2002/11/language-as-vision-the-ocularcentrism-of-chomskyan-linguistics-by-chris-werry/
677. Chris Werry. "Reflections on language: Chomsky, linguistic discourse and the value of rhetorical self-consciousness". *Language Sciences* 2007, 29:1, pp.66-87.
678. George Wolf. "First steps in syntax". George Wolf (ed.). *New Departures in Linguistics*. New York: Garland, 1992. pp.116-134.
679. George Wolf. "Real people doing real things in real time". *Language & Communication* 1997, 17:4, pp.359-368.

680. George Wolf. "Strawson on Chomsky". *Language Sciences* 1998, 20:4, pp.429-439.
681. George Wolf. "Quine and the segregational sign". *Language & Communication* 1999, 19:1, pp.27-43.
682. George Wolf. "Variations on a notational theme". *Language Sciences* 2002, 24:1, pp.57-71.
683. George Wolf and Nigel Love. "Integrational linguistics: an introductory survey". André Crochetière. Jean-Claude Boulanger & Conrad Ouellon (eds.), *Actes du XVe Congrès international des linguistes : Québec, Université Laval, 9-14 août 1992 : les langues menacées = Proceedings of the XVth International Congress of Linguists : Québec, Université Laval, 9-14 August 1992 : Endangered languages.* Quebec: Université Laval Press, 1993. 1, pp.313-320.
684. Ladislav Zgusta. Review of Michael Toolan. *Total Speech: An Integrational Linguistic Approach to Language.* Durham and London: Duke University Press, 1996. *Studies in the Linguistic Sciences* 1997, 27:2, pp.183-188.
685. ZHANG Tian Shirly. *The Importance of Being 'in Time': An Integrational Linguistic Approach.* MPhil dissertation, The University of Hong Kong, 2014.
686. ZHOU Feifei. *System, Order, Creativity: Models of the Human in Twentieth-Century Linguistic Theories.* PhD dissertation, The University of Hong Kong, 2014.

D. Descriptive linguistics.

For Harris's pre-integrationist studies, see 16, 28, 33, 36, 46, 50 and 58 in Part I.

687. David Bade. Review of Marcel Erdal, Irina Nevskaya and Astrid Menz (eds.), *Areal, Historical and Typological Aspects of South Siberian Turkic.* Wiesbaden: Harrassowitz Verlag, 2012. *Mongolian Studies* 2011, 33, pp.119-125.

688. David Bade. Review of Robert Binnick. *The Past Tenses of the Mongolian Verb: Meaning and Use.* Leiden: Brill, 2012. **Mongolian Studies** 2011, 33, pp.127-135.
689. David Bade. Review of Elisabetta Ragagnin. *Dukhan, a Turkic Variety of Northern Mongolia: Description and Analysis.* Wiesbaden: Harrassowitz, 2011. (Turcologica, 76) **Mongolian Studies** 2011, 33, pp.141-146.
690. Jesper Hermann. "Hvorfor savnes søsters næse. Anmeldelse af Hanne Ruus: *Danske kerneord. Centrale dele af den danske leksikalske norm I-II*". **Nydanske Sprogstudier** 1997, 23, pp.107-122.
691. Christopher Hutton and Kingsley Bolton. *A Dictionary of Chinese Slang: the Language of Hong Kong Movies, Street Gangs and City Life.* Honolulu: University of Hawai'i Press, 2005. xxiv + 492 pp.
692. Jacques Legrand. *Parlons mongol.* Paris: L'Harmattan, 1997. 413 pp.
693. Nigel Love. *Generative Phonology: a Case-study from French.* Amsterdam: John Benjamins, 1981. 241pp.
694. George Wolf, Michèle Bocquillon, Debbie de la Houssaye, Phyllis Krzyzek, Clifton Meynard, Lisbeth Philip. "Pronouncing French names in New Orleans". **Language in Society** 1996, 25:3 pp.407-426. Reprinted in Roy Harris and George Wolf (eds.). *Integrational Linguistics: a First Reader.* Oxford: Pergamon, 1998. pp.324-341.

E.   Cognitive linguistics. Biology. Evolution

For writings by Roy Harris, see 95, 106, 126-128, 130, 215, 238, 254, 292 and 312 in Part I.

695. James D. Benson, Meena Debashish, William S. Greaves, Jennifer Lukas, Sue Savage-Rumbaugh, Jared Taglialatela. "Mind and brain in apes: a methodology for phonemic

analysis of vocalizations of language competent bonobos". *Language Sciences* 2004, 26:6, pp.643-660.
696. Wayne Christensen. "Self-directedness, integration and higher cognition". *Language Sciences* 2004, 26:6, pp.661-692.
697. Andy Clark. "Is language special? Some remarks on control, coding, and co-ordination". *Language Sciences* 2004, 26:6, pp.717-726.
698. Stephen J. Cowley. "The baby, the bathwater and the "language instinct" debate". *Language Sciences* 2001, 23:1, pp.69-91.
699. Stephen J. Cowley. "Why brains matter: an integrational perspective on *The Symbolic Species*". *Language Sciences* 2002, 24:1, pp.73-95. Corrigenda: *Language Sciences* 2002, 24:3-4, p.491.
700. Stephen J. Cowley. "Simulating others: the basis of human cognition?". *Language Sciences* 2004, 26:3, pp.273-299.
701. Stephen J. Cowley. "Contextualizing bodies: human infants and distributed cognition". *Language Sciences* 2004, 26:6, pp.565-591.
702. Stephen J. Cowley. "Bridges to history: biomechanical constraints in language". Nigel Love (ed.). *Language and History: Integrationist Perspectives.* London and New York: Routledge, 2006. pp.200-222.
703. Stephen J. Cowley. "The cognitive dynamics of distributed language". *Language Sciences* 2007: 29:5, pp.575-583.
704. Stephen J. Cowley. "Distributed language: biomechanics, functions, and the origins of talk." *Emergence of Communication and Language.* London: Springer, 2007. pp.105-127.
705. Stephen Cowley. "Cognitive dynamics: language as values realizing activity". Alexander Kravchenko (ed.), *Cognitive Dynamics in Linguistic Interactions.* Newcastle upon Tyne: Cambridge Scholars Publishing, 2012. pp.1-32.

706. Steve Farrow. "Text world theory and cognitive linguistics". *Language & Communication* 2008, 28:3, pp. 276-281.
707. Laurence Goldstein. "Philosophical integrations". *Language Sciences* 2004, 26:6, pp.545-563.
708. Alexander V. Kravchenko. "The ontology of signs as linguistic and non-linguistic entities: a cognitive perspective". *Annual Review of Cognitive Linguistics* 2003, 1, pp.179-191.
709. Alexander V. Kravchenko. "Whence the autonomy? A reply to Harnad and Dror". *Pragmatics & Cognition* 2007, 15:3, pp.587-597.
710. Alexander V. Kravchenko. *Biology of Cognition and Linguistic Analysis: From Non-Realist Linguistics to a Realistic Language Science*. Frankfurt/Main etc.: Peter Lang, 2008.
711. Alexander V. Kravchenko. "'Everything said is said by an observer': the cognitive distinction between the infinitive/participle clausal arguments". Jean-Rémi Lapaire, Guillaume Desagulier, Jean-Baptiste Guignard (eds.), *Du fait grammatical au fait cognitif = From Gram to Mind : Grammar as Cognition.* Pessac: Presses Universitaires de Bordeaux, 2008. pp.267-284.
712. Alexander V. Kravchenko. "The experiential basis of speech and writing as different cognitive domains". *Pragmatics & Cognition* 2009, 17:3, pp.527-548.
713. Alexander V. Kravchenko. "How Humberto Maturana's biology of cognition can revive the language sciences". *Constructivist Foundations* 2011, 6:3, pp.227-237.
714. Alexander Kravchenko. "Grammar as semiosis and cognitive dynamics". Alexander Kravchenko (ed.), *Cognitive Dynamics in Linguistic Interactions.* Newcastle upon Tyne: Cambridge Scholars Publishing, 2012. pp.125-153.

715. Александр Владимирович Кравченко. "Биологическая реальность языка." *Вопросы когнитивной лингвистики* 2013, 1, pp.55-63.
716. Per Linell. "Dialogical language, dialogical minds, dialogical brains: is there a convergence between dialogism and neuro-biology?" *Language Sciences* 2007, 29:5, pp.605-620.
717. Per Linell. "Formal written-language-biased vs. dialogical linguistics on the nature of language". Alexander Kravchenko (ed.), *Cognitive Dynamics in Linguistic Interactions.* Newcastle upon Tyne: Cambridge Scholars Publishing, 2012. pp.125-153.
718. Nigel Love. "Cognition and the language myth". *Language Sciences* 2004, 26:6, pp.525-544.
719. Peter Mühlhäusler. "Talking about environmental issues". *Language & Communication* 1983, 3:1, pp.71-82.
720. Peter Mühlhäusler. "The interdependence of linguistic and biological diversity". David Myers (ed.), *The Politics of Multiculturalism in Oceania and Polynesia.* Darwin: University of the Northern Territories, 1995. pp.154-161.
721. Adriano Palma. "Automaticity". *Language Sciences* 2004, 26:6, pp. 609-619.
722. Don Ross. "Metalinguistic signalling for coordination amongst social agents". *Language Sciences* 2004, 26:6, pp.621-642.
723. E. Sue Savage-Rumbaugh, Stuart G. Shanker and Talbot J. Taylor. "Apes with language". *Critical Quarterly* 1996, 38:3, pp.45-57.
724. Sue Savage-Rumbaugh, Stuart G. Shanker and Talbot J. Taylor. *Apes, Language and the Human Mind.* New York: Oxford University Press, 1998. vii + 244 pp.
725. Stuart G. Shanker. "Ape language in a new light". *Language & Communication*, Special Issue on "Primate Communication" (B.J. King, guest editor), 1994, 14:1, pp.59-86.

726. Stuart G. Shanker, E.Sue Savage Rumbaugh and Talbot J. Taylor. "Kanzi A new beginning". *Animal Learning & Behavior* 1999, 27:1, pp.24-25.
727. David Spurrett. "Distributed cognition and integrational linguistics". *Language Sciences* 2004, 26:6, pp.497-501.
728. John Sutton. "Representation, levels, and context in integrational linguistics and distributed cognition". *Language Sciences* 2004, 26:6, pp.503-524.
729. Talbot J. Taylor. "The anthropomorphic and the sceptical". *Language & Communication*, Special Issue on "Primate Communication" (B.J. King, guest editor), 1994, 14:1, pp.115-127.
730. Talbot J. Taylor. "The origin of language: why it never happened". *Language Sciences* 1997, 19:1, pp.67-78.
731. Talbot J. Taylor and Stuart G. Shanker. "Ape Linguistics (Or: is Kanzi a Cartesian?)". David Cram, Andrew Linn, and Elke Nowak (eds), *The History of Linguistics, 1996*. Amsterdam, John Benjamins, 1999. (Studies in the History of the Language Sciences, 94) pp.57-70.
732. Talbot J. Taylor and S.G. Shanker. "The significance of ape language research". D. Johnson and C. Erneling (eds.), *The Mind as a Scientific Object*. New York: Oxford University Press, 2005. pp.367-380.
733. Chris Werry. "Rhetoric and reflexivity in cognitive theories of language". *Language & Communication* 2005, 25:4, pp.377-397.
734. Michael Wheeler. "Is language the ultimate artefact?" *Language Sciences* 2004, 26:6, pp.693-715.

F. History. Historical Linguistics. History of Linguistics

For writings by Roy Harris see 54, 76, 99, 274, 282 and 298 in Part I.
For book reviews of Harris's writings on history, see 487-492 in Part II.

735. Sylvain Auroux. *La révolution technologique de la grammatisation: introduction à l'histoire des sciences du langage*. Liège: Mardaga, 1994. (Philosophie et langage) 216 pp.
736. David Bade. *Of Palm Wine, Women and War: the Mongolian Naval Expedition to Java in the 13th Century.* Singapore: Institute for Southeast Asian Studies Press, 2013. xx + 320 pp.
737. Philip Carr, Patrick Honeybone. "English phonology and linguistic theory: an introduction to issues, and to 'Issues in English Phonology'". **Language Sciences** 2009, 29:2-3, pp.117-153.
738. Tony Crowley. "A history of 'the history of the language'". **Language & Communication** 1986, 6:4, pp.293-303.
739. Tony Crowley. "The return of the repressed: Saussure and Swift on language and history". George Wolf (ed.). *New Departures in Linguistics*. New York: Garland, 1992. pp.1236-249.
740. Geoffrey Galt Harpham. "Language and prehistory". Nigel Love (ed.). *Language and History: Integrationist Perspectives.* London and New York: Routledge, 2006. pp.188-199.
741. Anthony Holiday. "Positivism revisited: the philosophical semantics of Ayer's *Language, Truth and Logic*". Roy Harris (ed.), *Linguistic Thought in England, 1914-1945*. London: Duckworth, 1988. pp.165-191.

742. Anthony Holiday. "Forgiving and forgetting: the Truth and Reconciliation Commission". Sarah Nuttall and Carli Coetzee (eds.), *Negotiating the Past: The Making of Memory in South Africa*, Cape Town: Oxford, 1998. pp.43-56.
743. Paul Hopper. "Was Bakhtin a Proto-Integrationist?" Paper presented at MLA 1999. Available at: http://www.academia.edu/4005271/Bakhtin_as_Integrationalist_MLA_
744. Werner Hüllen. Review of Christopher M. Hutton, *Linguistics and the Third Reich*. **Historiographia Linguistica** 2000, 27:1, pp.162–175.
745. Christopher Hutton. "Noyekh Prilutski: philosopher of language." D.-B. Kerler (ed.). *History of Yiddish Studies*. Chur, Switzerland: Harwood, 1991. (Winter Studies in Yiddish, vol. 3) pp. 15-23.
746. Christopher M. Hutton. *Linguistics and the Third Reich: Mother-Tongue Fascism, Race and the Science of Language*. London and New York: Routledge, 1999. (Routledge Studies in the History of Linguistics, 1) x + 416 pp.
747. Christopher M. Hutton. "In the shadows of the Third Reich: case study of a dialectologist". **Historiographia Linguistica** 2000, 27:1, pp.127-136.
748. Christopher M. Hutton. "The search for a total dictionary of Chinese". (Editor's Introduction). S. Wells Williams. *Syllabic Dictionary of the Chinese Language*. London, UK: Ganesha, 2001. pp.v-xxv.
749. Christopher Hutton. "Word-stories: etymology as history". Nigel Love (ed.). *Language and History: Integrationist Perspectives.* London and New York: Routledge, 2006. pp.60-70.
750. Christopher M. Hutton. "The Romantic theory of language: writing and speech in Western views of the

Chinese language". *Critical Zone: A Forum of Chinese & Western Knowledge* 2006, 2, pp.82-105.
751. Christopher M. Hutton. "Fictions of affinity and the Aryan paradigm". Markus Messling and O. Ette, (eds.), *Wort Macht Stamm: Rassismus und Determinismus in der Philologie (18./19. Jh.)*. Paderborn: Wilhelm Fink Verlag, 2013. pp.89-106.
752. John E. Joseph. "Bloomfield's Saussureanism". *Cahiers Ferdinand de Saussure* 1989, 43, pp.43-53. Reprinted in John Fought (ed.), *Leonard Bloomfield: Critical Assessments of Leading Linguists*, vol. 2: *Reviews and Meaning*. London and New York: Routledge, 1999. pp.200-209.
753. John E. Joseph. "Ideologizing Saussure: Bloomfield's and Chomsky's readings of the *Cours de linguistique générale*". John E. Joseph and Talbot J. Taylor (eds.). *Ideologies of Language*. London and New York: Routledge, 1990. pp.51-78.
754. John E. Joseph, Nigel Love, Talbot J. Taylor. *Landmarks in Linguistic Thought II: The Western Tradition in the Twentieth Century*. London and New York: Routledge, 2001.
755. John E. Joseph, Nigel Love, Talbot J. Taylor. "Harris on linguistics without languages". John E. Joseph, Nigel Love, Talbot J. Taylor (eds.), *Landmarks in Linguistic Thought II: The Western Tradition in the Twentieth Century*. London and New York: Routledge, 2001. pp.203-218.
756. John E. Joseph. "'The grammatical being called a nation': history and the construction of political and linguistic nationalism". Nigel Love (ed.). *Language and History: Integrationist Perspectives*. London and New York: Routledge, 2006. pp.120-141.
757. Roger Lass. "The end of linear narrative? Reflections on the historiography of English". Nigel Love (ed.). *Language*

and History: Integrationist Perspectives. London and New York: Routledge, 2006. pp.19-40.
758. Nigel Love. "The linguistic thought of J.R. Firth". Roy Harris (ed.), *Linguistic Thought in England, 1914-1945.* London: Duckworth, 1988. pp.148-164.
759. Nigel Love. "The language myth and historical linguistics". Roy Harris (ed.). *The Language Myth in Western Culture.* London: Curzon, 2002. pp.25-40.
760. Nigel Love. "Language, history and *Language and History*". Nigel Love (ed.). *Language and History: Integrationist Perspectives.* London and New York: Routledge, 2006. pp.1-18.
761. Peter Mühlhäusler. "Humboldt, Whorf and the roots of ecolinguistics". Martin Pütz and Marjolijn Verspoor (eds.), *Explorations in Linguistic Relativity.* Amsterdam: John Benjamins, 2000. pp.89-100.
762. Anne-Marie-Anne Paveau. "Analyse du discours et histoire: rencontres et oublis". Simone Bonnafous and Malika Temmar (eds.). *Analyse du discours et sciences humaines et sociales.* (Chemins du discours) Paris: Ophrys, 2007. pp.121-134.
763. Antonio Perri. "Los folios 44 recto y verso del Codice Telleriano-Remensis y la historia colonial de los Mexica". ***Itinerarios*** 2008, 8, pp.129-151.
764. Rupert T. Pickens and Wendy Pfeffer. "In memoriam George Wolf." ***Tenso*** 2002, 17:2, pp.71-72.
765. Othmar Plöckinger. "Linguistics and the Third Reich". ***Language Sciences*** 2001, 23:6, pp.715-724.
766. Jerzy Szymura. "Bronislaw Malinowski's 'ethnographic theory of language'". Roy Harris (ed.), *Linguistic Thought in England, 1914-1945.* London: Duckworth, 1988. pp.106-131.
767. Talbot J. Taylor. "The place of Charles Bally in the Lockean tradition". H. Aarsleff et al. (eds.), *Papers in the*

History of Linguistics. Philadelphia: John Benjamins, 1987. pp.607-614.
768. Talbot J. Taylor. "The Theory of Speech and Language d'Alan Gardiner. Une pragmatique empirique". *Modèles linguistiques* 1987, 9:2, pp.101-118. French translation of the following item.
769. Talbot J. Taylor. "Alan Gardiner's *The Theory of Speech and Language*: empiricist pragmatics". Roy Harris (ed.), *Linguistic Thought in England, 1914-1945.* London: Duckworth, 1988. pp.132-147.
770. Talbot J. Taylor. "Locke on the imperfection of language". ***Newsletter for the Henry Sweet Society for the History of Linguistic Ideas*** 1988, 11, pp.6-8.
771. Talbot J. Taylor. "Condillac: language as an analytic method". *Language & Communication* 1989, 9:4, pp.289-297.
772. Talbot J. Taylor. "Free will vs. arbitrariness in the history of the linguistic sign". Hans-Josef Niederehe and Konrad Koerner (eds). *History and Historiography of Linguistics.* Amsterdam: John Benjamins, 1990. pp.79-89.
773. Talbot J. Taylor. "Liberalism in Lockean linguistics". ***Historiographia Linguistica*** 1990, 17:1/2, pp.99-109. Reprinted in F. Dineen (ed.), *North American Perspectives in Linguistic Historiography.* Amsterdam and Philadelphia: John Benjamins, 1990.
774. Talbot J. Taylor. "Talking about what happened". Nigel Love (ed.). *Language and History: Integrationist Perspectives.* London and New York: Routledge, 2006. pp.156-171.
775. Michael Toolan. "Part of the meaning/history of *euro*: integrational corpus linguistics". Nigel Love (ed.). *Language and History: Integrationist Perspectives.* London and New York: Routledge, 2006. pp.172-187.
776. Michael R. Walrod. "Language: object or event? The integration of language and life". Nigel Love (ed.).

Language and History: Integrationist Perspectives. London and New York: Routledge, 2006. pp.71-78.
777. Edda Weigand. "Indeterminacy of meaning and semantic change". Nigel Love (ed.). *Language and History: Integrationist Perspectives*. London and New York: Routledge, 2006. pp.79-98.
778. George Wolf. "C.K. Ogden". Roy Harris (ed.), *Linguistic Thought in England, 1914-1945*. London: Duckworth, 1988. pp.85-105.
779. George Wolf. "Translator's introduction: the emergence of the concept of semantics". Michel Bréal. *The Beginnings of Semantics: Essays, Lectures and Reviews*. Edited and translated by George Wolf. London: Duckworth; Stanford: Stanford University Press, 1991. pp.3-18.
780. Wolf, George. Review of Bertil Malmberg. *Histoire de la linguistique de Sumer à Saussure*. **Historiographia Linguistica** 1992, 19:1, pp.169-176.
781. George Wolf. "A glance at the history of linguistics. Saussure and historical-comparativism". Sheila Embleton, John E. Joseph and Hans-Josef Niederehe (eds.), *The Emergence of the Modern Language Sciences: Studies on the Transition from Historical-Comparative to Structural Linguistics in Honour of E.F.K. Koerner. Volume 1: Historiographical Perspectives*. Amsterdam: John Benjamins, 1999. pp.129-137.
782. George Wolf. "Are we all Saussureans now?" **Historiographia Linguistica** 2000, 27:2-3, pp.359-377.
783. Wolf, George. "The importance of Panini for the development of the science of meaning". Harjeet Singh and Giovanni Manetti (eds.), *Signs and Signification* v.2 (special issue of **Language Forum** 26:1-2). New Delhi: Bahri Publications, 2000. pp.29-40.

G. Writing. Literacy

For writings by Roy Harris, see 41, 93, 101, 132, 134, 157, 158, 178, 184, 193, 204, 207, 223, 224, 229, 233, 243, 246, 250, 253, 269-270, 275, 290, 323, 326, 329 in Part I.

For book reviews of Harris's writings on writing, see 378-387, 422-437, 461-472, 484, 508-511 in Part II.

784. Anis, Jacques. "Vers une sémiolinguistique de l'écrit". *Linx* 2000, 43 (Linguistique de l'écrit, linguistique du texte), pp.29-44. URL : http://linx.revues.org/1046 ; DOI : 10.4000/linx.1046
785. Naomi S. Baron. "Commas and canaries: the role of punctuation in speech and writing". *Language Sciences* 2001, 23:1, pp.15-67.
786. Annette Béguin-Verbrugge. *Images en texte, images du texte : dispositifs graphiques et communication écrite.* Villeneuve-d'Ascq: Presses universitaires du Septentrion, 2006. 313 pp.
787. Jens Brockmeier, David R. Olson, Min Wang. *Literacy, Narrative and Culture*. Richmond: Curzon, 2002. (World of writing) vi + 314pp. Reprinted: London and New York: Routledge, 2013.
788. Jerome Bruner. "Narrative distancing: a foundation of literacy". Jens Brockmeier, David R. Olson, Min Wang. *Literacy, Narrative and Culture*. Richmond: Curzon, 2002. pp.86-93.
789. Jesús Camarero. "Jean-Jacques Rousseau gramatólogo". *Cédille: revista de estudios franceses* 2009, 5, pp.81-105.
790. Michael Cloete. "Plato and Hountondji: philosophical discourse in an oral and literate cultural tradition". *Phronimon* 2012, 13:2, pp.73-98.
791. Djane Antonucci Correa. "Aspects of writing and identity". *Language Sciences* July 2011, 33:4, pp.667-672.

792. Martine Cotin. *L'écriture, l'espace*. Paris: L'Harmattan, 2005. (Espaces discursifs) 192pp.
793. Martine Cotin. *Scripturalité - Ecriture et pratiques culturelles*. Paris: Harmattan, 2009. (Nouvelles Etudes Anthropologiques) 209pp.
794. Jean Davallon (ed.). *L'économie des écritures sur le web. Vol 1: Les traces d'usage dans un corpus de sites de tourisme*. Paris : Hermès Sciences-Lavoisier, 2012. (Ingénierie représentationnelle et constructions de sens) 288pp.
795. Christopher M. Hutton. "Analysis and notation: the case for a non-realist linguistics". Rom Harré and Roy Harris (eds.), *Linguistics and Philosophy*. Oxford: Pergamon, 1993. pp.165-178. Reprinted in Roy Harris and George Wolf (eds.). *Integrational Linguistics: a First Reader*. Oxford: Pergamon, 1998. pp.241-251.
796. Jean-Marie Klinkenberg. "Entre servitude et autonomie. Quelle place pour l'écriture dans les sciences du langage?" **SHS Web of Conferences** 2014, 8 (4e Congrès Mondial de Linguistique Française) pp.45-64. http://www.shs-conferences.org/articles/shsconf/abs/2014/05/shsconf_cmlf 14_01397/shsconf_cmlf14_01397.html
797. Sybille Krämer. "Gibt es eine Sprache hinter dem Sprechen?" Herbert Ernst Wiegand (ed.). *Sprache und Sprachen in den Wissenschaften: Geshichte und Gegenwart. Festschrift für Walter de Gruyter & Co. anläßlich einer 250jährigen Verlagstradition*. Berlin and New York: Walter de Gruyter, 1999. pp.372-403.
798. Linell , Per. *The Written Language Bias in Linguistics: its Nature, Origins and Transformations*. London: Routledge, 2005.
799. Giovanni Lussu. *La lettera uccide: storie di grafica*. Roma: Stampa Alternativa ; Viterbo: Nuovi Equilibri, 1999. (Scritture, 7) 192pp.

800. Giovanni Lussu and Antonio Perri. "La scrittura e paradossi del visibile". *Il Verri* 1999, 44:10-11, pp. 52-62.
801. Sinfree B. Makoni. "'The Lord is my shock absorber': a socio-historical integrationist approach to mid 20th century literacy practices in Ghana". Angela Creese amd Adriana Blackledge (eds.), *Heteroglossia as a Practice and Pedagogy*. Heidelberg: Springer Publishing, 2014. (Educational Linguistics, 20) pp.1-21.
802. Richard Menary. "Writing as thinking" *Language Sciences* 2007, 29:5, pp.621-632.
803. Juan Carlos Moreno Cabrera. "The written language bias in linguistic typology". *Cuadernos de lingüística del I.U.I. Ortega y Gasse*t 2008, 15, pp.117-137. Available at: http://www.academia.edu/3205369/66._The_Written_Language_Bias_in_Linguistic_Typology_CUADERNOS_DE_LINGUISTICA_XV_2008_IUOG_pags._117-137
804. Peter Mühlhäusler. "'Reducing' Pacific languages to writings". John E. Joseph and Talbot J. Taylor (eds.). *Ideologies of Language*. London and New York: Routledge, 1990. pp.189-205.
805. David R. Olson. "A new mentality". George Wolf and Nigel Love (eds.), *Linguistics Inside Out*. Amsterdam: John Benjamins, 1997. pp.99-105.
806. David R. Olson, "What writing is". *Pragmatics and Cognition* 2001, pp.239-258.
807. Janette Pelletier. "Young children's "clever misunderstandings" about print". Jens Brockmeier, David R. Olson, Min Wang (eds.), *Literacy, Narrative and Culture*. Richmond: Curzon, 2002. pp.245-265.
808. Antonio Perri. "Processus cognitif et valeur artistique dans l'écriture aztèque". Joaquín Galarza (ed.), *Descifre de las escrituras mesoamericanas : códices, pinturas, estatuas, cerámica : Proceedings, 46 Congreso Internacional de Americanistas/International Congress of Americanists,*

Amsterdam, Netherlands, 1988. Oxford: BAR, 1989. (BAR international series, v. 518) vol. I, p. 25-44.
809. Antonio Perri. "Le medium et le message. Une approche sémiotique et anthropologique à l'étude des systèmes d'écriture". *Versus* 1994, 72 (Semiotics and the Effects-of-Media-Change Research Programmes), pp. 107-128.
810. Antonio Perri. "El reverso de la Conquista. Intertesto e contaminazioni nel f. 44v del Codex Telleriano-Remensis". **Thule. Rivista italiana di studi americanistici** 1999, 6/7, pp. 227-241.
811. Antonio Perri. "La forma del testo/2. Alcune considerazioni teoriche". S. Covino (ed.), *La scrittura professionale. Ricerca, prassi, insegnamento. Perugia, Università per Stranieri, 23-25 ottobre 2000*. Firenze: Olschki, 2001, vol. 1, pp. 69-81.
812. Antonio Perri. "Writing". A. Duranti (ed.), *Key Terms in Language and Culture*. Malden: Blackwell, 2001. pp. 272-274.
813. Antonio Perri. "L'immagine azteca: (anti)norma e trasposizioni". R. Contessi, M. Mazzeo, T. Russo (eds.), *Linguaggio e percezione*. Roma: Carocci, 2002. pp. 99-108.
814. Antonio Perri. "Tlacuiloa, scrivere dipingendo. Alcune osservazioni su fonetismo e simbolismo del colore nei codici aztechi". S. Beta, M. Sassi (eds.), *I colori nel mondo antico. Esperienze linguistiche e quadri simbolici*. Fiesole: Edizioni Cadmo, 2003. pp.89-100.
815. Antonio Perri. "Pintar sonidos. Hacia una explicación semiótica del "fonetismo" como rasgo intrínseco de la escritura azteca-náhuatl". *Atti del XXV Convegno Internazionale di Americanistica. Perugia - Xalapa, 9-11 maggio; 21-24 ottobre 2003*. Perugia: Argo Editrice, 2005. (Quaderni di Thule. Rivista italiana di studi americanistica) vol. 2, pp. 83-94.
816. Antonio Perri. "Trasposizione, segnale, metasemiotica (non scientifica). Spunti per una grafematica (post)hjelm-

sleviana e per una tipologia semiotica dei sistemi grafici".
R. Galassi, B. Morandina, C. Zorella (eds.), *Filosofia del linguaggio e semiotica. Janus, Quaderni del circolo glossematico*. Vicenza: Terra Ferma, 2007. pp.151-170.
817. Antonio Perri. "Tipologia dei sistemi grafici in chiave antropologica". Fabrizio Scrivano (ed.) *Re-lab: immagini parole: seminario sulle scritture*. Perugia: Morlacchi Editore, 2007. pp.73-92.
818. Antonio Perri. "Evento linguistico vs evento scrittorio: verso un nuovo modello". *Rivista di psicolinguistica applicata* 2007, VII, pp. 125-145.
819. Antonio Perri. "Insegnare la 'zona visio-grafica'". G. Fiorentino (ed.), *Scrittura e società. Storia cultura professioni*. Roma: Aracne, 2007. pp.149-174.
820. Antonio Perri. "Afterword. Reading without spirit?". ***Text & Talk*** 2008, 28:5, pp.691-698.
821. Antonio Perri. "Al di là della tecnologia, la scrittura: il caso Unicode". ***Annali*** (Università degli Studi Suor Orsola Benincasa) 2009, 14:2, pp.725-748.
822. Antonio Perri. "Il problema delle unità minime nella scrittura azteca. Contributo ad una teoria integrata della scrittura". ***Testo e senso*** 2010, no.11 http://testoesenso.it/article/view/4
823. Antonio Perri. "Apostrofe e ironia, tra dire e mostrare. Strategie dell'enunciazione visiva nella pittografia azteca del Codex Telleriano-Remensis". *Retorica del visibile. Strategie dell'immagine tra significazione e comunicazione. 2. Comunicazioni. Venezia, 13-16 aprile 2010*. Roma: Aracne, 2011. pp.73-90.
824. Antonio Perri. "Writing, image and linearity: the Aztec case". ***Progetto grafico*** 2011, 19, pp. 46-49.
825. Antonio Perri. "Quando è scrittura? Spunti per una riflessione semiotica su sistemi notazionali e grafismi". ***Annali*** (Università degli Studi Suor Orsola Benincasa), 2012, II, pp.101-129.

826. Antonio Perri. "Recensione a *Histoire de l'écriture. De l'idéogramme au multimédia*, sous la direction de Anne-Marie Christin. Paris, Flammarion, 2012. (seconda edizione aumentata)". *Testo e senso* 2012, no.13 Available at: http://testoesenso.it/article/view/111/118
827. Antonio Perri. "Tra spazio bianco e "horror vacui". Critica della "ragione grafica" come trasposizione (del parlato) e soglia critica (del grafismo)". *Il Verri* 2013, 53, pp.13-35.
828. Antonio Perri. "Los Mandamientos de la Ley de Dios. Multigrafismo y sincretismos escriturales en el f. 8r del Manuscrito Egerton 2898". M.A. Ruz Barrio and J.J. Batalla Rosado (eds.), *Códices del Centro de México. Análisis Comparativos y Estudios Individuales*. Warszawa: Universytet Warszawki Wydział "Artes Liberales", 2013. pp.359-395.
829. Antonio Perri. "Repertori grafici e scrittori. Un modello integrato applicato a contesti storico-antropologici controversi". Marco Mancini and Barbara Turchetta (eds.), *Etnografia della scrittura*. Roma: Carocci Editore, 2014. pp.263-324.
830. Antonio Perri. "Why writing is not (only) transcribing? Writing codes in contact: steps towards multigraphic literacy practices". *Testo & senso* 2014, 15, pp.75-98.
831. Oliver Timken Perrin. "Tamgas and space: territorial mark and mnemotechnic". Joám Evans Pim, Sergey A. Yatsenko, Oliver Timken Perrin, (eds.), Caroline Humphrey (advising editor), *Traditional Marking Systems: A Preliminary Survey*. London & Dover: Dunkling Books, 2010. pp.
832. Oliver Timken Perrin. "Marks: a distinct category within writing as integrationally defined". **Language Sciences** July 2011, 33:4, pp.623-633.
833. Oliver Timken Perrin. "The mark of commerce: uncertainty in mark predication". ***Re:marks*** 2013, 1, pp.127-161.

834. Oliver Timken Perrin, Joám Evans Pim, Sergey A. Yatsenko. "Mark studies: an interdisciplinary approach". Joám Evans Pim, Sergey A. Yatsenko, Oliver Timken Perrin, (eds.), Caroline Humphrey (advising editor), *Traditional Marking Systems: A Preliminary Survey.* London & Dover: Dunkling Books, 2010. pp.7-21.
835. John Sören Pettersson. "Phonography: setting a term to the evolution of writing". George Wolf and Nigel Love (eds.), *Linguistics Inside Out*. Amsterdam: John Benjamins, 1997. pp.84-98.
836. Joám Evans Pim. "From marks to ogham: rethinking writing in Gallaecia". *Re:marks* 2013, 1, pp.89-126.
837. Joám Evans Pim, Sergey A. Yatsenko, Oliver Timken Perrin, (eds.), Caroline Humphrey (advising editor). *Traditional Marking Systems: A Preliminary Survey.* London & Dover: Dunkling Books, 2010. 518pp.
838. Frank Salomon, comments by Hilda Araujo, Roy Harris, Walter D. Mignolo and Gary Urton. "How an Andean 'writing without words' works." ***Current Anthropology*** 2001, 42:1, pp.1-27.
839. Fabrizio Scrivano (ed.). *Re-lab: immagini parole: seminario sulle scritture*. Perugia: Morlacchi Editore, 2007. 162 pp.
840. Fabio Schiavino. "Scrittura e suono: una simbiosi conflittuale". Fabrizio Scrivano (ed.) *Re-lab: immagini parole: seminario sulle scritture*. Perugia: Morlacchi Editore, 2007. pp.57-64.
841. Colette Sirat. "Quelques réflexions sur l'écriture et la paléographie". ***Gazette du livre médiéval*** 1994, 24, pp.25-29.
842. Emmanuël Souchier. "Quelques remarques sur le sens et la servitude de la typographie". ***Cahiers GUTenberg*** 2006, 46-47, pp. 69-98.
http://cahiers.gutenberg.eu.org/fitem?id=CG_2006___46-47_69_0

843. Barbara Turchetta and Antonio Perri. "Codici interferiti". Marco Mancini and Barbara Turchetta (eds.), *Etnografia della scrittura*. Roma: Carocci Editore, 2014. pp.325-361.
844. Julian Warner. "Studying writing". **Journal of Documentation** 1997, 53, pp.226-237. Reprinted in his *Information, Knowledge, Text*. Lanham MD: Scarecrow Press, 2001. pp.1-16.
845. George Wolf. "Writing for the twenty-first century". **Language Sciences** 1997, 19:1, pp.93-100.
846. Alessandro Zinna. *Le interfacce degli oggetti di scrittura: teoria del linguaggio e ipertesti*. Roma: Meltemi, 2004. 311pp.
847. Alessandro Zinna. "The object of writing". **Language Sciences** July 2011, 33:4, pp.634-646.

H.   Education. Language learning and teaching

For writings be Roy Harris on education, see 293 (2) and 325 in Part I.

848. David Balosa. "Three examples of better English learning through the L1". **TESOL Essential Teacher** 2006, 3:1. Available online: http://www.tesol.org/read-and-publish/journals/other-serial-publications/compleat-links/compleat-links-volume-3-issue-1-(march-2006)/three-examples-of-better-english-learning-through-the-l1
849. Daniel R. Davis. "Teaching American English as a foreign language: an integrationist approach". M. Hayhoe and S. Parker (eds.) *Who Owns English?* Buckingham & Philadelphia: Open University Press, 1994. pp.68-76. Reprinted in Roy Harris and George Wolf (eds.). *Integrational Linguistics: a First Reader*. Oxford: Pergamon, 1998. pp.305-312.

850. Daniel R. Davis. "Language learning, grammar and integrationism". Michael J. Toolan (ed.) *Language Teaching: Integrational Linguistic Approaches*. New York & London: Routledge, 2009. pp.73-87.
851. Christopher M. Hutton. "Grammaticality and the English teacher in Hong Kong: an integrationist analysis". Michael J. Toolan (ed.) *Language Teaching: Integrational Linguistic Approaches*. New York & London: Routledge, 2009. pp.88-103.
852. Christopher M. Hutton. "The 'worldliness' of English, hostility to English-medium education among missionaries in China, and 'china English'." Hans-Georg Wolf, Lothar Peter and Frank Polzenhagen (eds.) *Focus On English: Linguistic Structure, Language Variation And Discursive Use: Studies in Honour of Peter Lucko*. Leipzig: Leipzig University Press, 2008. pp.81-92.
853. Peter E. Jones. "Bernstein's 'codes' and the linguistics of 'deficit'". **Language and Education** 2013, 27:2, pp.161-179.
854. Rukmini Bhaya Nair. "Learning to write: integrational linguistics and the Indian subcontinent". Michael J. Toolan (ed.) *Language Teaching: Integrational Linguistic Approaches*. New York & London: Routledge, 2009. pp.47-72.
855. Mark Evan Nelson and Richard Kern. "Language teaching and learning in the *postlinguistic condition?*" Lubna Alsagoff, Sandra Lee Mckay, Guangwei Hu, Willy A. Renandya (eds.) *Principles and Practices for Teaching English as an International Language*. New York: Routledge, 2012. (ESL & Applied Linguistics Professional Series) pp.47-66.
856. Jon Orman and Adrian Pablé. "Polylanguaging, integrational linguistics and contemporary sociolinguistic theory: a commentary on Ritzau". *International Journal of*

Bilingual Education and Bilingualism 2015 (published online 1 April 2015) DOI:10.1080/13670050.2015.1024606
857. Charles Owen. "Integrational linguistics and language teaching". Michael J. Toolan (ed.) *Language Teaching: Integrational Linguistic Approaches*. New York & London: Routledge, 2009. pp.156-176.
858. Sally Pryor. "Integrationism, new media art and learning to read Arabic". Michael J. Toolan (ed.) *Language Teaching: Integrational Linguistic Approaches*. New York & London: Routledge, 2009. pp.104-119.
859. Michael J. Toolan. "Language teaching and integrational linguistics". Michael J. Toolan (ed.) *Language Teaching: Integrational Linguistic Approaches*. New York & London: Routledge, 2009. pp.1-23.
860. Michael J. Toolan. "Assessing students' writing: just more grubby verbal hygiene?" Michael J. Toolan (ed.) *Language Teaching: Integrational Linguistic Approaches*. New York & London: Routledge, 2009. pp.140-155.
861. Leo van Lier. *The Ecology and Semiotics of Language Learning: a Sociocultural Perspective*. Dordrecht: Kluwer Academic Publishers, 2004. pp.264.
862. Edda Weigand. "Teaching a foreign language: a tentative enterprise". Michael J. Toolan (ed.) *Language Teaching: Integrational Linguistic Approaches*. New York & London: Routledge, 2009. pp.120-139.
863. Ruihan Zhang. "Identity, culture, and language: putting SLA back in context?" *The Asian Conference on Language Learning 2012. Official Conference Proceedings 2012. Osaka, Japan*. Nagoya, Japah: iafor, 2012. pp.68-74. Available at http://iafor.org/offprints/acll2012-offprints/ACLL2012_offprint_0055.pdf

I. Translation

For writings by Roy Harris on translation see 31, 39, 43, 85, 109, 122, 337 (34) in Part I.

864. John E. Joseph. "Indeterminacy, translation and the law". Marshall Morris (ed.), *Translation and the Law*. Amsterdam & Philadelphia: John Benjamins, 1995. (American Translators Association Scholarly Monograph Series, 8.) pp.13-36.
865. John E. Joseph. "Harris's Saussure, Harris as Saussure: the translations of the *Cours* and the *Third Course*". ***Language Sciences*** July 2011, 33:4, pp.524-530.
866. Alan Melby. "Machine translation and philosophy of language". ***Machine Translation Review*** April 1999, 9, pp.6-17.
867. Marshall Morris. "What problems? On learning to translate". George Wolf (ed.). *New Departures in Linguistics*. New York: Garland, 1992. pp.199-212. Reprinted in George Wolf (ed.). *New Departures in Linguistics*. New York: Garland, 1992. pp. 313-323.
868. Douglas Robinson. *Performative Linguistics: Speaking and Translating as Doing Things with Words*. London: Routledge, 2003. 260 pp.
869. Michael R. Walrod and Jamin R. Pelkey. "Four faces, eight places: elaborate expression, emergent meaning, and translation as discourse art". ***Journal of Translation*** 2010, 6:1, pp.11-26.

J. Literature

For Roy Harris's early writings on literature, see Part I; for his integrationist writings, see 155, 191, 306 in Part I.

870. David Bade. "Imaginary travels in post-socialist Mongolia". *Inner Asia* 2013, 15:1, pp.135-164.
871. Kingsley Bolton and Christopher M. Hutton. "Orientalism, linguistics and Postcolonial Studies". *Interventions* 2000, 2, pp.1-5.
872. David Eisenschitz. *Lectures linguistique et humoristique en ?Adab Sāxir: les livres de Omer Taher et Haitham Dabbour en Égypte contemporaine (2005-2011)*. Mémoire en vue de l'obtention du Master 2 Recherche, Université Paris-La Sorbonne, Département/U.F.R. des études araes et hébraîiques, 2014.
873. Christopher M. Hutton. "Race and language: ties of 'blood and speech', fictive identity and empire in the writings of Henry Maine and Edward Freeman". *Interventions* 2000, 2, pp.53-72.
874. Ana Mercedes Pedrazzini. *La construction de l'image présidentielle dans la presse satirique: vers une grammaire de l'humour. Jacques Chirac dans l'hebdomadaire français* **Le Canard enchaîné** *et Carlos Menem dans le supplément argentin Sátira/12*. Université Paris-Sorbonne, Universidad de Buenos Aires, Facultad de Ciencias Sociales, École doctorale V, Concepts et langages, Laboratoire de recherche GRIPIC. Thèse our obtenir le grade de Docteur de l'Université Paris-Sorbonne en Sciences de l'information et de la communication, Docteur de l'Uiversité de Buenos Aires en sciences sociales, 2010. 684 pp. Available at: http://www.e-sorbonne.fr/sites/www.e-sorbonne.fr/files/theses/These_finale_PEDRAZZINI_Ana_11-2010.pdf

875. Emmanuelle Pelard." Le nomadisme du signe dans les « pseudographies » de Christian Dotremont et d'Henri Michaux". *Cygne Noir: revue d'exploration sémiotique* 2013 nr.1 http://www.revuecygnenoir.org/numero/article/le-nomadisme-du-signe-dotremont-michaux
876. Emmanuel Souchier. "Formes et pouvoirs de l'énonciation éditoriale". *Communication et langages* 2007 154, pp. 23-38.
877. Talbot J. Taylor. *Linguistic Theory and Structural Stylistics.* Oxford: Pergamon Press, 1981. (Language & Communication Library, 2) vii + 111pp.
878. Talbot J. Taylor. "Communication and literary style". *Poetics Today* 1982, 3:4, pp.39-51.
879. Talbot J. Taylor and Michael J. Toolan. "Recent trends in stylistics". *Journal of Literary Semantics* 1984, 13:1, pp.57-79. Reprinted in J.-J. Weber (ed.), *The Stylistics Reader*. London: Arnold, 1996.
880. Michael Toolan. "Analyzing fictional dialogue". *Language & Communication* 1985, 5:3, PP.193-206. Reprinted in Roy Harris and George Wolf (eds.). *Integrational Linguistics: a First Reader*. Oxford: Pergamon, 1998. pp.209-223.
881. Michael Toolan. *Narrative: a Critical Linguistic Introduction*. London and New York: Routledge, 1988. (INTERFACE) xviii, 282 pp.
882. Michael Toolan. *Narrative: a Critical Linguistic Introduction*. Second Edition. London and New York: Routledge, 2001. (The INTERFACE Series) xii + 260 pp.
883. Kyoko Takashi Wilkerson and Douglas Wilkerson. "The Gloss as Poetics: Transcending the Didactic". *Visible Language* 2000, 34:3, pp.228-262.

K. Arts

For writings by Roy Harris on the arts, see 197, 203, 219, 271, 304, 334 in Part I.

For book reviews of Harris's writings on the arts, see 485, 486, 514 in Part II.

884. William Conger. "Abstract painting and integrational linguistics". *Language Sciences* July 2011, 33:4, pp.654-661.
885. Abigail Diamond. "The role of the art object in contemporary art". *Working Papers in Art and Design* 3 Available at: https://www.herts.ac.uk/__data/assets/pdf_file/0015/12354/WPIAAD_vol3_diamond.pdf
886. Envoy Enterprises. "THE GREAT DEBATE ABOUT ART on view at Envoy Enterprises 87 Rivington Street 25 January - 8 March 2015" http://envoyenterprises.tumblr.com/post/110081518639/the-great-debate-about-art-on-view-at-envoy
887. Stella Harvey. "Who's afraid of Serotaspeak?" *Language & Communication* 2004, 24:3, pp.241-268.
888. Charlotte Bisgaard Nielsen. "Perception som forståelsens grundlag: Monet og Cézannes forskninger". Jesper Hermann, Charlotte Bisgaard Nielsen, Maarja Siiner (eds.). *På sporet af sprogpsykologi: 12 artikler om sproglighedens psykologi*. København: Frydenlund, 2005. pp.15-26.
889. Trevor Pateman. "Language, art and Kant". George Wolf and Nigel Love (eds.), *Linguistics Inside Out*. Amsterdam: John Benjamins, 1997. pp.226-228.
890. Perra Loca. "America the beautiful?" Michael Hernandez de Luna, *American Beauty*. Chicago: Bad Press Books, 2008, pp.134-135.

891. Sally Pryor. *Extending integrationist theory through the creation of a multimedia work of art: Postcard from Tunis.* Unpublished doctoral thesis, University of Western Sydney, 2003. Available at http://www.sallypryor.com/thesis.html
892. Sally Pryor. "Postcards and supasigns: extending integrationist theory through the creation of interactive digital artworks". ***Human Technology*** 2007, 3:1, pp.54-67.
893. Sally Pryor. "Who's afraid of integrationist signs? Writing, digital art, interactivity and integrationism". ***Language Sciences*** July 2011, 33:4, pp.647-653.
894. Anna Tietze. "The language myth and western art". Roy Harris (ed.), *The Language Myth in Western Culture.* London: Curzon, 2002. pp.183-200.
895. George Wolf. "The language myth, Schopenhauer and music". Roy Harris (ed.), *The Language Myth in Western Culture.* London: Curzon, 2002. pp.201-220.

L.   Psychology. Communication

For Roy Harris's writings on psychology and communication see 55, 64, 86, 140, 202, 236, 293(1), 328(16, 17), 342(53) in Part I.

896. Louis S. Berger. *Averting Global Extinction: Our Irrational Society as Therapy Patient.* Plymouth UK: Jason Aronson, 2009. 140 pp.
897. Charlotte Conrad. "Efter sprogmytens fald – tekstforståelse som subjekts- og kontekstafhængig erkendelse". Anne Mette Hansen og Karen Skovgaard-Petersen (eds.), *Betydning & Forståelse. Festskrift til Hanne Ruus.* København: Selskab for Nordisk Filologi, Københavns Universitet, 2013. pp.313-324.
898. Dorthe Duncker. "Som at gå i Jesus' fodspor". Marianne Rathje and Linda Svenstrup (eds.), *Sprogpsykologi:*

udvalgte kerneemner. København: Museum Tusculanum, 2004. pp.201-220.
899. Dorthe Duncker. "Den integrerende kommunikationsmodel". P. Widell and M. Kunøe (eds.), *10. Møde om udforskningen af dansk sprog: Aarhus Universitet 7.-8. oktober 2004*. Århus: Institut for Nordisk Sprog og Litteratur, Aarhus Universitet, 2005. pp.137-146.
900. Bent Holshagen Hemmingsen. ""Forankringer og forventninger: hukommelse overfor læring og forståelse." *Spindet* 2009, 9:1, pp.19-32.
901. Bent Holshagen Hemmingsen. "Interaktionsstudier i en George Jetson tid". *Spindet* 2010, 10:1, 45-46.
902. Jesper Hermann. "How acquainting shows verbally." *Language Sciences* 2004, 26:6, pp.593–607.
903. Jesper Hermann. "The language problem". *Language & Communication* 2008, 28:1, pp.93–99.
904. Jesper Hermann. "Integrating the persons communicating: towards a lay-oriented science of communication--defining the research agenda". *Language Sciences* July 2011, 33:4, pp.575-578.
905. Jesper Hermann. Dorthe Duncker, Anne Mette Hansen og Karen Skovgaard-Petersen (eds.), *Betydning & Forståelse. Festskrift til Hanne Ruus*. København: Selskab for Nordisk Filologi, Københavns Universitet, 2013. pp.351-360.
906. Hoyois, Laure. *An integrational perspective on interpersonal encounters: Research on communication exchanges between Hong Kong taxi drivers and Westerners*. Unpublished M.A. dissertation. University of Lausanne, 2010.
907. Peter E. Jones. "From 'external speech' to 'inner speech' in Vygotsky: A critical appraisal and fresh perspectives". *Language & Communication* 2009, 29:2, pp.166-181.
908. Peter E. Jones and Chick Collins. "Political analysis versus Critical Discourse Analysis in the treatment of

ideology: some implications for the study of communication." *Atlantic Journal of Communication* 2006, 14:1-2, pp.28-50.
909. Krzysztof Korżyk. "The integrative and structuring function of speech in face-to-face communication from the perspective of human-centered linguistics." A. Esposito, M. Bratanić, E. Keller (eds.). *Fundamentals of Verbal and Nonverbal Communication and the Biometric Issue.* Amsterdam and Washington, DC: IOS Press, 2007. (NATO security through science series. E, Human and societal dynamics ; v. 18) pp.92-99.
910. Gavan Lintern. "Cognitive systems and communication". *Language Sciences* July 2011, 33:4, pp.708-712.
911. Charlotte Marie Bisgaard Nielsen. *Sprog der ikke kommunikerer - integrationismens centrale kommunikationssynspunkt som grundlag for en sprogpsykologisk analyse af kampagnen som meddelelsessituation med eksempel i Sundhedsstyrelsens succeskampagne i uge 40.* Master's thesis, Københavns Universitet, 2002.
912. Charlotte Marie Bisgaard Nielsen. "'... for det var ikke det vi lærte noget om. Det var formerne' (BEAT online cutup machine)". *Spindet* 2009, 9:1, pp.9-18.
913. Charlotte Marie Bisgaard Nielsen. "Towards applied integrationism: integrating autism in teaching and coaching sessions". *Language Sciences* July 2011, 33:4, pp.593-602.
914. Charlotte Marie Bisgaard Nielsen. "'Think Human' – Om baggrunden for uge 40 kampagnens dommedagsprofeti: 'kommunikationsdesign' og 'maskintænkning'". *Spindet* 2012, 12:1, pp.12-19. English translation by David Bade available online: "'Think Human' – What does that mean in a communication perspective?" http://www.academia.edu/2970694/Think_Human
915. Charlotte Marie Bisgaard Nielsen. *Integrating the mind - an analysis of the metaphorical terminology in autism research.* 1 udg. Guldbæk: Anvendt Ny Integrationel

Lingvistik, 2013. 26 pp.
http://www.academia.edu/5551877/Integrating_the_mind_-_an_analysis_of_the_metaphorical_terminology_in_autism_research

916. Charlotte Marie Bisgaard Nielsen. *Contextualizing aquired brain damage*. (Conference abstract). Guldbæk: Anvendt Ny Integrationel Lingvistik, 2014. 22 pp. Available at: http://www.academia.edu/7502554/Contextualizing_aquired_brain_damage

917. Adrian Pablé. "Human decision-making is unpredictable. Insights from integrational linguistics". ***Rassegna Italiana di Linguistica Applicata*** 2013, 45:2-3, pp.35-39.

918. Stuart Shanker and Talbot J. Taylor. "The house that Bruner built". D. Bakhurst, & S. Shanker (eds.), *Jerome Bruner: Language, Culture, Self.* London: SAGE Publications, 2001. pp.50-71.

919. John R. Taylor. "Linguistic theory and the multiple-trace model of memory". George Wolf and Nigel Love (eds.), *Linguistics Inside Out*. Amsterdam: John Benjamins, 1997. pp.208-225.

920. Talbot J. Taylor. "Linguistic origins: Bruner and Condillac on learning how to talk". ***Language & Communication*** 1984, 4:4, pp.209-224.

921. Talbot J. Taylor. "Folk psychology and the language myth: what would the integrationist say?" Roy Harris (ed.), *The Language Myth in Western Culture.* London: Curzon, 2002. pp. 100-117.

922. Talbot J. Taylor. "Where does language come from? The role of reflexive enculturation in language development". ***Language Sciences*** 2010, 32:1, pp.14-27.

923. Talbot J. Taylor. "Language development and the integrationist". ***Language Sciences*** July 2011, 33:4, pp.579-583.

924. Talbot J. Taylor. "Understanding others and understanding language: how do children do it?" *Language Sciences* 2012, 34, pp.1-12.
925. Talbot J. Taylor and Stuart Shanker. "Rethinking language acquisition: what the child learns". Hayley G. Davis and Talbot J. Taylor (eds.). *Rethinking Linguistics.* London and New York: Routledge, 2003. pp.151-170.
926. Toolan, Michael. "An integrational linguistic view of coming into language." J.H. Leather and Jet van Dam (eds.). *Ecology of language acquisition.* Dordrecht: Kluwer Academic Publishers, 2003. (Educational Linguistics ; v.1) pp.123-139.
927. Jaime Ernesto Vargas Mendoza. "Integrational linguistics and the behavioral sciences". *Language Sciences* July 2011, 33:4, pp.584-592.
928. Michael R. Walrod. "The role of emotions in normative discourse and persuasion". Edda Weigand (ed.). *Emotion in Dialogic Interaction.* Amsterdam: John Benjamins, 2004. pp.211-223.
929. Michael R. Walrod. "Cultural and contextual constraints in communication". Marion Grein and Edda Weigand (eds.), *Dialogue and Culture.* Amsterdam: John Benjamins, 2007. pp.239-256.
930. Line Brink Worsøe. "What's in a word, what's a word in?" *Language Sciences* July 2011, 33:4, pp.603-614.
931. Zhang Ruihan Cathy. *Rethinking Vygotsky: A Critical Reading of Vygotsky's Cultural-Historical Theory and Its Appropriation in Contemporary Scholarship.* MPhil dissertation, The University of Hong Kong, 2013.

M. Anthropology. Ethnology

For writings by Roy Harris on anthropology see especially no.326 in Part I.

932. Kingsley Bolton and Christopher M. Hutton. "Bad Boys and Bad Language: *chou hau* and the sociolinguistics of swearing in Hong Kong". G. Evans and S.M.M. Tam (eds.), *Hong Kong: The Anthropology of a Chinese Metropolis*. London: Curzon/The University of Hawaii Press, 1997. pp.299-331.
933. Steve Farrow. "Language and culture". ***Language & Communication*** 2004, 24:3, pp. 269-274.
934. Christopher M. Hutton. "The critique of primitive belief and modern linguistics". ***Journal of Literary Semantics*** 1995, 24, pp.81-103.
935. Christopher M. Hutton. "From pre-modern to modern: Ethnic classification by language and the case of the Ngai/Nung of Vietnam". ***Language & Communication*** 1998, 18:2, pp.125-132.
936. Christopher M. Hutton. "Cultural and conceptual relativism, universalism and the politics of linguistics". R. Dirven, B. Hawkins & E. Sandikcioglu (eds.). *Language and Ideology I: Cognitive Theoretical Approaches*. Amsterdam: John Benjamins, 2001. pp.277-296.
937. Christopher Hutton. *Race and the Third Reich: Linguistics, Racial Anthropology and Genetics in the Dialectic of Volk*. Cambridge: Polity, 2005. vii + 272 pp.
938. Christopher M. Hutton. "Human diversity and the genealogy of languages: Noah as the founding ancestor of the Chinese". ***Language Sciences*** 2008, 30:5, pp.512-528.
939. Christopher M. Hutton. "Nazi race theory and belief in an "Aryan race": a profound failure of interdisciplinary communication". ***The International Journal of Science in Society*** 2010, 1:4, pp.149-156.

940. Christopher M. Hutton and Kingsley Bolton. "Linguistics in cross-cultural communication: From the Chinese Repository to the 'Chinese Emerson'". *Journal of Asian Pacific Communication* 2000, 9, pp.145-163.
941. Christopher M. Hutton and Kingsley Bolton. "Media mythologies: the case of triad language". C. Barron, N. Bruce, and D. Nunan (eds.). *Knowledge and Discourse*. London: Longman, 2002. pp.147-163.
942. Yves Jeanneret. "Complexité de la notion de trace. De la traque au tracé". Béatrice Galinon-Mélénec (ed.). *L'Homme trace: Perspectives anthropologiques des traces contemporaines*. Paris: CNRS Éditions, 2011. pp.59-86.
943. Peter Mühlhäusler. "Nature and nurture in the development of Pidgin and Creole languages". Martin Pütz and René Dirven (eds.), *Wheels Within Wheels*. Frankfurt: Peter Lang, 1989. pp.33-54.
944. George Wolf. "Malinowski's 'context of situation'". *Language & Communication* 1989, 9:4, pp.259-267.

N. Sociolinguistics. Politics. Economics

For writings by Roy Harris on politics see especially nos. 144 and 341(50) in Part I.

945. Kingsley Bolton and Christopher M. Hutton. "Bad and banned language: triad secret societies, the censorship of the Cantonese vernacular, and colonial language policy in Hong Kong". *Language in Society* 1995, 24:2, pp.159-186.
946. Deborah Cameron. "Sexism and semantics". *Radical Philosophy* 1984, 36, pp.14-16. Reprinted in her *On Language and Sexual Politics*. London and New York: Routledge, 2006. pp.13-18.
947. Deborah Cameron. "What has gender got to do with sex?" *Language & Communication* 1985, 5:1, pp.19-28. Reprinted in Roy Harris and George Wolf (eds.).

Integrational Linguistics: a First Reader. Oxford: Pergamon, 1998. pp.273-282.
948. Deborah Cameron. *Feminism and Linguistic Theory*. London: Macmillan/New York: St Martins, 1985. ix + 195 pp. 2nd edition, 1992, x + 247 pp.
949. Deborah Cameron. "Demythologizing sociolinguistics: why language does not reflect society". John E. Joseph and Talbot J. Taylor (eds.). *Ideologies of Language*. London and New York: Routledge, 1990. pp.79-93.
950. Deborah Cameron. "New arrivals" the feminist challenge in language study". George Wolf (ed.). *New Departures in Linguistics*. New York: Garland, 1992. pp.213-235.
951. Deborah Cameron. *Verbal Hygiene*. London and New York: Routledge, 1995. (The Politics of Language Series) xvi + 264 pp.
952. Deborah Cameron. "When worlds collide: expert and popular discourse on language". **Language Sciences** 1997, 19:1, pp.7-13.
953. Tony Crowley. "Description or prescription? An analysis of the term 'standard english' in the work of two twentieth-century linguists". **Language & Communication** 1987, 7:3, pp.199-220
954. Tony Crowley. *The Politics of Discourse: The Standard Language Question in British Cultural Debates*. Basingstoke: Macmillan Education, 1989. vi + 302 pp. United States edition published as *Standard English and the Politics of Language*. Urbana: University of Illinois Press, 1989.
955. Tony Crowley. "Uniform, excellent, common: reflections on standards in language". **Language Sciences** 1997, 19:1, pp.15-21.
956. Hayley G. Davis. "Theorising women's and men's language". **Language & Communication** 1996, 16:1, pp.71-79.

957. Hayley G. Davis. "Gender, discourse, and *Gender and Discourse*". ***Language & Communication*** 1997, 17:4, pp.353-357.
958. Hayley G. Davis. "What makes bad language bad?" ***Language & Communication*** 1989, 9:1, pp.1-9. Reprinted in Roy Harris and George Wolf (eds.). *Integrational Linguistics: a First Reader*. Oxford: Pergamon, 1998. pp.283-293.
959. Hayley G. Davis. "Typography, lexicography and the development of the idea of 'standard English'". T. Bex and R. Watts (eds.), *Standard English: The Widening Debate*. London: Routledge, 1999 pp.69-88.
960. Hayley G. Davis. Review of Deborah Cameron. *Good to Talk? Living and Working in a Communication Culture*. London and New Delhi: Sage Publications, 2000. ***Language & Communication*** 2001, 21:4, pp.381-384.
961. Hayley G. Davis. "The language myth and standard English". Roy Harris (ed.). *The Language Myth in Western Culture*. London: Curzon, 2002. pp.41-54.
962. Margaret Deuchar. "Feminism and linguistic theory". ***Language & Communication*** 1987, 7:1, pp.77-81.
963. Caroline Henton. "The abnormality of male speech". George Wolf (ed.). *New Departures in Linguistics*. New York: Garland, 1992. pp.27-59.
964. Anthony Holiday. "Language and liberation". ***Language & Communication*** 1987, 7:1, pp.81-90.
965. Christopher M. Hutton. "Normativism and the notion of authenticity in Yiddish linguistics". D. Goldberg (ed.). *The Field of Yiddish: Studies in Language, Folklore, and Literature. Fifth Collection*. Evanston, Ill. : Northwestern University Press ; New York : YIVO Institute for Jewish Research, 1993. pp. 11-57.
966. Christopher M. Hutton. "The language myth and the race myth: evil twins of modern identity politics?" Roy Harris

(ed.). *The Language Myth in Western Culture*. London: Curzon, 2002. pp.118-138.
967. Christopher M. Hutton. "Linguistics and nationalism". *Encyclopedia of Language & Linguistics* (Second Edition), Amsterdam: Elsevier, 2006. v. 8, pp.485-488.
968. Christopher M. Hutton. "Language as identity in language policy discourse: reflections on a political ideology". Kirsten Süselbeck, Ulrike Mühlschlegel, Peter Masson (eds.). *Lengua, Nación e Identidad: La Regulación del Plurilingüismo en España y América Latina*. Berlin: Bibliotheca Ibero-Americana/Vervuert, 2008. pp.75-87.
969. Christopher M. Hutton. "Vernacular spaces and >non-places< : dynamics of the Hong Kong linguistic landscape". Markus Messling, Dieter Läpple, Jürgen Trabant (eds.), *Stadt und Urbanität: Transdisziplinäre Perspektiven.* Berlin: Kulturtverlag Kadmos, 2011. (The new metropolis - Die neue Metropole, Volume 0/2010) pp.162-184.
970. Peter E. Jones. "Why there is no such thing as 'critical discourse analysis'". ***Language & Communication*** 2007, 27:4, pp.337-368.
971. Peter E. Jones. "Signs of activity: integrating language and practical action". ***Language Sciences*** 2011, 33:1, pp.11-19.
972. Peter E. Jones. "Value for money? Putting Marx through the mill". ***Language Sciences*** July 2011, 33:4, pp.689-694.
973. Peter E. Jones and Chik Collins. "State ideology and oppositional discourses." Michael Huspek (ed.). *Oppositional Discourses and Democracies*. New York: Routledge, 2010. pp.17-39.
974. John E. Joseph. Review of Bambi B. Schieffelin, Kathryn A. Woolard and Paul V. Kroskrity (eds.), *Language Ideologies: Practice and Theory*. New York and Oxford: Oxford University Press, 1998. ***Journal of Multilingual and Multicultural Development*** 1999, 20, pp.253-255.

975. Nigel Love, Umberto Ansaldo. "The native speaker and the mother tongue". *Language Sciences* 2010, 32:6, pp.589-593.
976. Sinfree B. Makoni. "Sociolinguistics, colonial and postcolonial: an integrational perspective". *Language Sciences* July 2011, 33:4, pp.680-688.
977. Sinfree B. Makoni. "A critique of language, languaging and supervernacular = Uma crítica à noção de língua, linguagem e supervernáculo". *Muitas Vozes* 2012, 1:2, pp.189-199.
978. Sinfree B. Makoni. "An integrationist perspective on colonial linguistics". *Language Sciences* 2013, 35, pp.87-96.
979. Sinfree B. Makoni and Alistair Pennycook. "Disinventing and reconstituting languages". S. Makoni & A. Pennycook (eds), *Disinventing and Reconstituting Languages*. Clevedon: Multilingual Matters, 2007. pp.1-41.
980. Robert McColl Millar. "On the cusp: Antoine Meillet as a sociologist of language". Nigel Love (ed.). *Language and History: Integrationist Perspectives.* London and New York: Routledge, 2006. pp.99-119.
981. Juan Carlos Moreno Cabrera. "Linguistic structure and social structure". *Journal of Multicultural Discourses* 2006, 1:2, pp.115-120.
982. Juan Carlos Moreno Cabrera. "Gramáticos y academias: para una sociología del conocimiento de las lenguas = Grammarians and academies: towards a sociology of linguistic knowledge". *Arbor: Ciencia, Pensamiento y Cultura* 2008, CLXXXIV:731, pp.519-528. Available at: http://arbor.revistas.csic.es/index.php/arbor/article/view/201/201
983. Juan Carlos Moreno Cabrera. "La manipulación de la lingüística al servicio del nacionalismo españolista. El caso del andaluz en la fonología de la *Nueva gramática* de la

RAE y la Asale". *Actas, VI reunión de escritores/as en Andaluz*. Málaga: Z.E.A, 2012. pp.3-29.
984. Peter Mühlhäusler. "Patterns of contact, mixture, creation and nativization: their contribution to a general theory of language". Charles-James N. Bailey and Roy Harris (eds.), *Developmental Mechanisms of Language*. Oxford: Pergamon, 1985. (Language & Communication Library, 6) pp.51-88.
985. Peter Mühlhäusler. "Redefining creolistics". George Wolf (ed.). *New Departures in Linguistics*. New York: Garland, 1992. pp.193-198.
986. Peter Mühlhäusler. *Linguistic Ecology: Language Change and Linguistic Imperialism in the Pacific Region*. London and New York: Routledge, 1996. (The Politics of Language Series) 396 pp.
987. Peter Mühlhäusler. *Language of Environment, Environment of Language: a Course in Ecolinguistics*. London: Battlebridge, 2003. iv + 228 pp.
988. Peter Mühlhäusler. "Some notes on the ontology of Norf'k". **Language Sciences** July 2011, 33:4, pp.673-679.
989. Joshua Nash, Jon Orman. "Things people speak?: a response to Orman's 'Linguistic diversity and language loss: a view from integrational linguistics' with rejoinder". **Language Sciences** 2014, 41, Part B, pp.222-226.
990. Jon Orman. "Not so super: The ontology of 'supervernaculars'". **Language & Communication** 2012, 32:4, pp.349-357.
991. Jon Orman. "New lingualisms, same old codes". **Language Sciences** 2013, 37, pp.90-98.
992. Jon Orman. "Linguistic diversity and language loss: a view from integrational linguistics". **Language Sciences** 2013, 40, pp.1-11.
993. Adrian Pablé. "The 'dialect myth' and socio-onomastics. The names of the castles of Bellinzona in an integrational

perspective". ***Language & Communication*** 2009, 29:2, pp.152-165.
994. Adrian Pablé. "Excommunicated on the grounds of Harrisy. Roy Harris, linguistics and freedom of speech". Wayne Finke and Leonard Ashley (eds.*) Language under Controls: Policies and Practices Affecting Freedom of Speech*. New York: Cummings & Hathaway, 2012. pp.1-12.
995. Adrian Pablé. "Who wants Swiss English? Why a 'lay-oriented' sociolinguistics matters". ***English Today*** 2013, 29:3, pp.26-33.
996. Adrian Pablé. "The most misunderstood title in the world? Recontextualizing Roy Harris' inaugural lecture 'The worst English in the world?'". Michael O'Sullivan, David Huddart & Carmen Lee (eds.). *The Future of English in Asia*. London/New York: Routledge, 2015.
997. Adrian Pablé and Marc Haas. "Essentialism, codification and the sociolinguistics of identity". Karen Junod and Didier Maillat (eds.) *Performing the Self*. Tübingen: Narr Verlag, 2010. (SPELL. Swiss Papers in English Language and Literature, 24) pp.33-46.
998. Adrian Pablé, Marc Haas and Noel Christe. "Language and social identity: an integrationist critique". ***Language Sciences*** 2010, 32:6, pp.571-576.
999. Alistair Pennycook. "Postmodernism and language policy". T. Ricento (ed), *An Introduction to Language Policy: Theory and Method*. Oxford: Blackwell, 2006. pp.60-76.
1000. Alistair Pennycook. "Language-free linguistics and linguistics-free languages". Ahmar Mahboob and Naomi Knight (eds.), *Questioning Linguistics*. Newcastle upon Tyne: Cambridge Scholars Publishing, 2008. pp.18-31.
1001. Dieter Stein. "On the role of language ideologies in linguistic theory and practice: purism and beyond." Nils Langer, Winifred V. Davies (eds.), *Linguistic Purism in the*

Germanic Languages. Berlin: De Gruyter, 2005. (Studia linguistica Germanica, 75) pp. 188-204.

O. Religion

For writings by Roy Harris on religion see 155 and 293(15) in Part I.

1002. Andrew James Harvey. "Immortal signs: science, sacrament, and the poetics of immortality". ***Language & Communication*** 2006, 26:3-4, 369-380.
1003. Christopher M. Hutton. "Vernacular lexicography in the missionary context". Editor's Introduction in S. Wells Williams. *Tonic Dictionary of the Chinese Language in the Canton Dialect.* Ed. by Christopher M. Hutton. London, UK: Ganesha, 2001. pp. v-xxxi.
1004. Christopher M. Hutton and John E. Joseph. "Back to Blavatsky: the impact of theosophy on modern linguistics". ***Language & Communication*** 1988, 18:3, pp.181–204.
1005. Gabriel Levy. "Prophecy, written language, and the mimetic faculty: Benjamin's linguistic mysticism as cure of the "language myth". ***Epoché: The University of California Journal for the Study of Religion*** 2006, 24, pp.19-48.
1006. Gabriel John Levy. *Changing Channels: Biblical Prophecy, Writing, and Cognition.* Dissertation (Ph.D.), University of California, Santa Barbara, 2007. 219 pp. Available from ProQuest.
1007. Gabriel Levy. "Rabbinic language from an integrationist perspective". ***Language Sciences*** July 2011, 33:4, pp.695-707.
1008. Stanley E. Porter. "How do we know what we think we know? Methodological reflections on Jesus research". James H. Charlesworth, with Brian Rhea (eds.), *Jesus Research: New Methodologies and Perceptions : The*

Second Princeton-Prague Symposium On Jesus Research, Princeton 2007. Grand Rapids, Michigan: William B. Eerdmans Publishing Company, 2014. (Princeton-Prague Symposia series on the historical Jesus, 2) pp.82-99.

P.   Law

For writings by Roy Harris on law see 310 in Part I.

For book reviews of Harris and Hutton's *Definition in Theory and Practice*, see 498-504 in Part II.

1009. David Bade. Review of Chris Hutton. *Language, Meaning and the Law*. Edinburgh: Edinburgh University Press, 2009. ***Journal of Documentation*** 2011, 67:4, pp.731-738.
1010. Kingsley Bolton, Christopher Hutton, Peter Ip Pau-Fuk. "The speech-act offence: claiming and professing membership of a triad society in Hong Kong". ***Language & Communication*** 1996, 16:3, pp.263-290.
1011. Ronald R. Butters. Review of Christopher M. Hutton. *Language, Meaning and the Law*. Edinburgh: Edinburgh University Press, 2009. ***Journal of Sociolinguistics*** 2011, 15:4, p.532-537.
1012. Daniel R. Davis. "Trade mark law: Linguistic issues". ***Language & Communication*** 1996, 16:3, pp.255-262.
1013. Hayley Davis and Nigel Love. "Language and the law: Linguistics to the rescue?" ***Language & Communication*** 1996, 16:3, pp.301-313.
1014. Kirsty Duncanson. Review of Christopher M. Hutton. *Language, Meaning and the Law*. Edinburgh: Edinburgh University Pres, 2009. ***International Journal for the Semiotics of Law - Revue internationale de Sémiotique juridique*** June 2012, 25:2, pp.283-287.

1015. Alan Durant. "Circulation and stability: Language, law and money in Chris Hutton's *Language, Meaning and the Law*". ***Language & Communication*** 2009, 29:4, pp.394-400.
1016. Christopher Hutton. "Law lessons for linguists? Accountability and acts of professional communication". ***Language and Communication*** 1995, 16:3, pp.205-214. Reprinted in Roy Harris and George Wolf (eds.). *Integrational Linguistics: a First Reader*. Oxford: Pergamon, 1998. pp.294-304.
1017. Christopher Hutton. "Authority and expertise in forensic linguistics". ***Language & Communication*** 2005, 25:2, pp.183-188.
1018. Christopher M. Hutton. "Meaning, time and the law: Ex post and ex ante perspectives". ***International Journal For The Semiotics Of Law*** 2009, 22:3, pp.279-292
1019. Christopher Hutton. *Language, Meaning and the Law*. Edinburgh: Edinburgh University Pres, 2009. xii + 244 pp.
1020. Christopher Hutton. "Who owns language? Mother tongues as intellectual property and the conceptualization of human linguistic diversity". ***Language Sciences*** 2010, 32:6, pp.638-647.
1021. Christoher Hutton. "Objectification and transgender jurisprudence: the dictionary as quasi-statute". ***Hong Kong Law Journal*** 2011, 41, Part 1, pp.27-47.
1022. Christopher M. Hutton. "'I Crave the Law': Salomon v Salomon, uncanny personhood and the Jews". M. Wan (ed.), *Reading the Legal case: Cross-currents Between Law and the Humanities*. New York: Routledge, 2012. pp.29-46.
1023. Christopher M. Hutton. "Too obvious to translate? Legal formality and Chinese varieties in the Hong Kong magistrate's court". *The 2nd International Conference on Law, Translation and Culture (LTC2), Hong Kong, 31 May-2 June 2012.*

1024. Christopher M. Hutton. "Linguistic landscape, law and reflexive modernity". A. Wagner and R.K. Sherwin (eds.), *Law, Culture and Visual Studies*. Dordrecht; London: Springer, 2014. pp.599-613.
1025. Christopher M. Hutton. *Word Meaning and Legal Interpretation: An Introductory Guide*. Basingstoke: Palgrave, MacMillan, 2014. 243pp.
1026. John E. Joseph. "Integrational linguistics and the law". André Crochetière, Jean-Claude Boulanger, Conrad Ouellon, and Pierre Auger (eds.), *Actes du XVe Congrès International des Linguistes, Québec, Université Laval, 9-14 août 1992: Les langues menacées / Endangered Languages: Proceedings of the XVth International Congress of Linguists, Quebec, Université Laval, 9-14 August 1992*. Sainte-Foy: Presse Universitaire de Laval, 1993. v.1, pp.327-329.
1027. Ann Sinsheimer. "'English Only' and our struggle to understand the concept of language". **Language & Communication** 2005, 25:1, pp.61-80.
1028. Michael Toolan. "The language myth and the law". Roy Harris (ed.). *The Language Myth in Western Culture*. London: Curzon, 2002. pp.159-182.
1029. Michael Toolan. Review of Christopher M. Hutton. *Language, Meaning and the Law*. Edinburgh: Edinburgh University Pres, 2009. ***The International Journal of Speech, Language and the Law*** 2009, 16:2, p. 303-310.
1030. Iwona Witczak-Plisiecka. "A linguistic-pragmatic note on indeterminacy in legal language". ***Linguistica Copernicana*** 2009, 1:1, pp.231-243.
1031. Iwona Witczak-Plisiecka. "A note on the linguistic (in)determinacy in the legal context". ***Lodz Papers in Pragmatics*** 2009, 5:2, pp.201-226.

Q. Science. Mathematics

For writings by Roy Harris see 137, 224, 289, 293(14), 328(19) in Part I.

For book reviews of Harris's writings on science, see 483, 493-498 in Part II.

1032. Andreea S. Calude. "The science of numbers: does language help or hinder?". *Language Sciences* July 2011, 33:4, pp.562-568.
1033. Daniel R. Davis. "The language myth and mathematical notation as a language of nature". Roy Harris (ed.). *The Language Myth in Western Culture*. London: Curzon, 2002. pp.139-158.
1034. Rom Harré. "Integrating surrogationalism". *Language Sciences* July 2011, 33:4, pp.569-574.
1035. Anthony Holiday. "Science and significance: making sense of Wittgenstein's ways of seeing". George Wolf and Nigel Love (eds.), *Linguistics Inside Out*. Amsterdam: John Benjamins, 1997. pp.106-135.
1036. Alain Herreman. "Linguistique intégrationniste et histoire sémiotique des mathématiques". Accessed 10 September at: http://perso.univ-rennes1.fr/alain.herreman/linguistique_integrationniste.pdf
1037. Adrian Pablé. "Why the semantics of 'good' and 'bad' isn't good enough: popular science and the 'language crux'". *Language Sciences* July 2011, 33:4, pp.551-558.
1038. Nigel Sanitt. "A mingled yarn: problematology and science". *Revue internationale de philosophie* 2007, 4(no.242), pp.435-449.
1039. Nigel Sanitt. "Science and language". *Language Sciences* July 2011, 33:4 pp.559-561.
1040. David Spurrett. "Disintegrating Galileo: A Commentary on Pablé". *Social Epistemology Review and Reply*

Collective 10 December 2013, 3:1, pp.23-27. http://social-epistemology.com/2013/12/10/disintegrating-galileo-a-commentary-on-pable-david-spurrett/

R. Communication technologies. Communication at work. Human-computer interaction. Information science

For an essay by Roy Harris, see 207 in Part I.

1041. David Bade. *Misinformation and meaning in library catalogs.* Chicago: D. W. Bade, 2003. 295pp.
1042. David Bade. *The theory and practice of bibliographic failure, or, Misinformation in the information society.* Ulaanbaatar: Chuluunbat, 2004. 383pp.
1043. David Bade. "The Zheng He dilemma: language identification and automatic indexing". *Language & Communication* April 2006, 26:2, pp.193-199.
1044. David Bade. Review of Peter Janich. *Was ist Information? Kritik einer Legende.* Frankfurt am Main: Suhrkamp, 2006. *Journal of Documentation* 2008, 64:1, pp.172-174.
1045. David Bade. "Comparative review: Cognitive Systems". [Review of Erik Hollnagel and David D. Woods. *Joint Cognitive Systems: Foundations of Cognitive Systems Engineering.* Boca Raton, FL: CRC Press / Taylor & Francis, 2005; David D. Woods and Erik Hollnagel. *Joint Cognitive Systems: Patterns in Cognitive Systems Engineering.* Boca Raton, FL: CRC Press / Taylor & Francis, 2006] *Journal of Documentation* 2008, 64:6, pp.56-62.
1046. David Bade. "Colorless green ideals in the language of bibliographic description: making sense and nonsense in the library". *Language & Communication* January 2007, 27:1, pp.54-80.

1047. David Bade. "Relevance ranking is not relevance ranking, or, When the user is not the user, the search results are not search results". *Online Information Review* 2007, 31:6, pp.831-844.
1048. David Bade. Review of Michel Meyer. *Principia Rhetorica: une théorie générale de l'argumentation*. Fayard, 2008. *Journal of Documentation* 2009, 65:3, pp.515-522.
1049. David Bade. *Responsible librarianship: library policies for unreliable systems*. Duluth, Minnesota: Library Juice, 2008. xv + 172pp.
1050. David Bade. "Ethos, logos, pathos or Sender, message, receiver? A problematological rhetoric for information technology". *Cataloging & Classification Quarterly* 2009, 47:7, pp.612-630.
1051. David Bade. "Carlo Revelli on the (non)autonomy of cataloging. *Cataloging & Classification Quarterly* 2010, 48:8, pp.743-756.
1052. David Bade. "It's about time! Temporal aspects of metadata management in the work of Isabelle Boydens". *Cataloging & Classification Quarterly* 2011, 49:4, pp.328-338.
1053. David Bade. "Signs, language and miscommunication: an essay on train wrecks". *Language Sciences* July 2011, 33:4, pp.713-724.
1054. David Bade. "IT, that obscure object of desire: on French anthropology, museum visitors, airplane cockpits, RDA and the Next Generation Catalog". *Cataloging & Classification Quarterly* 2012 50:4, pp.316-334.
1055. David Bade. "Jakobsonian Library Science? A Response to Jonathan Tuttle's Article 'The Aphasia of Modern Subject Access'". *Cataloging & Classification Quarterly* 2013 51:4 pp.428-438.
1056. Jørgen P. Bansler, Erling C. Havn, Troels Mønsted and Kjeld Schmidt. "At the center of the galaxy: The integrative role of medical progress notes". G. Ellingsen and P. Bjørn

(eds.), *InfraHealth 2013: The 4th international workshop on Infrastructures for Healthcare: Action Research, Interventions, and Participatory Design, 13-14 June 2013, Tromsø, Norway, 2013*. Published online: http://site.uit.no/infrahealth/files/2013/06/Bansler_3.pdf

1057. Jørgen Bansler, Erling Havn, Troels Mønsted, Kjeld Schmidt, Jesper Hastrup Svendsen. "Physicians' progress notes: the integrative core of the medical record". O.W. Bertelsen, L. Ciolfi, M.A. Grasso, G.A. Papadopoulos (eds.), *ECSCW 2013: Proceedings of the 13th European Conference on Computer Supported Cooperative Work, 21-25 September 2013, Paphos, Cyprus 2013*. London: Springer, 2014. pp.123-142.

1058. Lars Rune Christensen. *The Coordination of Cooperative Work Through Artifacts*. MA Thesis, IT University of Copenhagen, March 2003. Available at: http://www.itu.dk/people/schmidt/teaching/theses/lrc_artifacts.pdf

1059. Lars Rune Christensen. 2007. "Practices of stigmergy in architectural work". Tom Gross, Kori Inkpen (eds.), *GROUP '07 Proceedings of the 2007 International ACM Conference on Supporting Group Work*. New York: ACM, 2007. pp.11-20.

1060. Lars Rune Christensen. *Coordinative Practices in the Building Process: An Ethnographic Perspective*. London and New York : Springer, 2013. (Computer Supported Cooperative Work) xvii + 135 pp.

1061. Dominique Cotte. *Des médias au travail. Emprunts, transferts, métamorphoses*, Habilitation à Diriger des Recherches, Université d'Avignon et des Pays du Vaucluse, 2007.

1062. Dominique Cotte. *Émergences et transformations des formes médiatiques*. Paris: Hermes-Science/Lavoisier, 2011. 272 pp.

1063. Sagun Dakhwa, Patrick A.V. Hall, Ganesh Bahadur Ghimire, Prakash Manandhar, and Ishwor Thapa. "Sambad – Computer Interfaces for Non-literates". J. Jacko (Ed.). *Human-Computer Interaction, Part I, HCII 2007* (LNCS 4550). Berlin: Springer, 2007. pp.721-730.

1064. Jan Davallon, Nathalie Noel-Cadet, and Danièle Brochu. "L'usage dans le texte: les "traces d'usage" du site Gallica." Emmanuël Souchier, Yves Jeanneret, and Joëlle Le Marec (eds.), *Lire, écrire, récrire: objets, signes et pratiques des médias informatisés*. Paris: Bibliothèque publique d'information, 2003. pp.47–89.

1065. Isabelle Garron, Jean-Luc Minel, Emmanuël Souchier. "Citer, indexer ou cartographier? De la circulation et de la lecture des textes relatifs à une ouvre littéraire sur internet". Ismaïl Timini and Susan Kovacs (eds.), *Indice, index, indexation : actes du colloque international organisé les 3 et 4 novembre 2005 à l'université de Lille-3 par les laboratoires CERSATES et GERICO*. (Paris : Association des professionnels de l'information et de la documentation (ADBS)) , v. 1 (2006): 163-174. Available at: http://hal.archives-ouvertes.fr/docs/00/08/28/52/PDF/ArticleFinal_IG_JLM_ES.pdf

1066. Ayan Ghosh, Lyuba Alboul, Jacques Penders, Peter Jones and Heath Reed. "Following a robot using a haptic interface without visual feedback." *ACHI 2014, The Seventh International Conference on Advances in Computer-Human Interactions*. 2014. pp.147-153. Accessed 11 September 2014 at: http://www.thinkmind.org/index.php?view=article&articleid=achi_2014_7_10_20072

1067. Claudia Henze. "Menneskelig kommunikation i midten af tekniske love". *Spindet* 2010, 10:1, pp7-10.

1068. Yves Jeanneret. *Y a-t-il (vraiment) des technologies de l'information?* Villeneuve d'Ascq: Presses Universitaires du

Septentrion, 2000. (Savoirs mieux. Communication, 10) 134 pp. 2nd ed.: Villeneuve d'Ascq: Presses Universitaires du Septentrion, 2007. (Collection Les savoirs mieux, 23) 200pp.

1069. Peter E. Jones. "You want a piece of me? Paying your dues and getting your due in a distributed world". *AI & Society* 2010, 25:4, pp.455-464.

1070. Peter Jones, Ayan Ghosh, Jacques Penders and Heath Read. "Towards human technology symbiosis in the haptic mode." *International Conference on Communication, Media, Technology and Design, 2-4 May 2013, Famagusta, North Cyprus.* Anadolu, 2013. pp.307-312. Accessed 11 September 2014 at: http://www.cmdconf.net/2013/Proceedings/Proceedings.pdf

1071. Camille Jutant. *S'ajuster, interpréter et qualifier une pratique culturelle: Approche communicationnelle de la visite muséale.* Uuniversité d'Avignon et des Pays de Vaucluse, École doctorale 537 – Culture et patrimoine. Université du Québec à Montréal, Programme international de doctorat conjoint en museologie, mediation et patrimoine. Thèse de doctorat conduite en vue de l'obtention des grades de : Docteur en sciences de l'information et de la communication & Philosophiæ doctor, Ph. D. 2011. 581 pp. Available at: http://tel.archives-ouvertes.fr/docs/00/81/92/39/PDF/THESE_-_Camille_-_Jutant_Avignon.pdf

1072. Nathalie Noel-Cadet. "La médiation comme mode d'approche des usages de l'Internet." *CIFSIC I-2003 X° colloque bilatéral franco-roumain, Université de Bucarest, 28 juin–3 juillet 2003.* 2003. http://archivesic.ccsd.cnrs.fr/docs/00/06/22/94/PDF/sic_000 00737.pdf

1073. Jacques Penders, Peter Jones, Anuradha Ranasinghe and Thrishantha Nanayakara. "Enhancing trust and confidence in human robot interaction." *UKRE*, Sheffield, 25 March

2013. Accessed 11 September 2014 at: http://shura.shu.ac.uk/6763/1/Penders-Reins[2].pdf
1074. Jacques Penders, Peter Jones, and Thrish Nanayakkara. "Exploring haptic interfacing with a mobile robot without visual feedback." *Advances in Autonomous Robotics*. Berlin and Heidelberg: Springer, 2012. (Lecture Notes in Computer Science, v.7429) pp.432-433.
1075. Kjeld Schmidt. *Cooperative Work and Coordinative Practices: Contributions to the Conceptual Foundations of Computer-Supported Cooperative Work (CSCW)*. New York and London : Springer, 2010. (Computer supported cooperative work) 488pp.
1076. Kjeld Schmidt and Ina Wagner. "Coordinative artifacts in architectural practice". Blay-Fornarino at al. (eds.) *Cooperative Systems Design: A Challenge of the Mobility Age*. [Proceedings of the Fifth International Conference on the Design of Cooperative Systems (COOP 2002), Saint Raphaël, France, 4- 7 June 2002]. Amsterdam: IOS Press, 2002. pp.257-274
1077. Kjeld Schmidt and Ina Wagner. "Ordering systems: coordinative practices and artifacts in architectural design and planning". **Computer Supported Cooperative Work** 2004, 13:5-6, 349–408.
1078. Kjeld Schmidt, Ina Wagner, Marianne Tolar. "Permutations of Cooperative Work Practices: A study of two oncology clinics". Tom Gross, Kori Inkpen (eds.), *GROUP 2007 Proceedings of the 2007 International ACM Conference on Supporting Group Work*. New York: ACM, 2007. pp. 1-10.
1079. Laurence Schmoll. "Le lecteur modèle des concepteurs de sites Internet pédagogiques". **Revue des Sciences Sociales** 2006, 36 (Écrire les sciences sociales), pp.68-75. Available at: http://www.eonautes.com/publications/SchmollL-2006-LecteurSitesPedag.pdf

1080. Bill Seaman. "Recombinant poetics and related database aesthetics". Viktorija Vesna Bulajić (ed.), *Database Aesthetics: Art in the Age of Information Overflow*. Minneapolis: University of Minnesota Press, 2007. pp.121-141.
1081. Emmanuël Souchier, Yves Jeanneret, and Joëlle Le Marec (eds.), *Lire, écrire, récrire: objets, signes et pratiques des médias informatisés*. Paris: Bibliothèque publique d'information, 2003. (Études et recherche). 352pp.
1082. Cécile Tardy, Jean Davallon and Yves Jeanneret. "Les médias informatisés comme organisation des pratiques de savoir". *Organisation des connaissances et société des savoirs : concepts, usages, acteurs. 6e colloque international du Chapitre français de l'ISKO*, 7-8 juin 2007 (2007): 169-184. Available at: http://www.isko-france.asso.fr/pdf/isko2007/Actes%20ISKO%20FR%202007%20p%20169-184.pdf
1083. Cécile Tardy and Yves Jeanneret (eds.). *L'écriture des médias informatisés : espaces de pratiques*. Paris: Hermes Science, 2007. (Coll. systèmes d'information et organisations documentaires) 222 pp.
1084. Julian Warner. "Semiotics, information science, documents and computers". ***Journal of Documentation*** 1990, 46:1, pp.16-32.
1085. Julian Warner. "Writing, programs, computers and logic". Kevin P. Jones (ed.), *Informatics 11: The Structuring of Information*. London: Aslib, 1991. pp.109-145.
1086. Julian Warner. "Writing and literary work in copyright: a binational and historical analysis". ***Journal of the American Society for Information Science*** 1993, 44:6, pp.307-321.
1087. Julian Warner. *From Writing to Computers*. London and New York: Routledge. 1994. ix + 159 pp.

1088. Julian Warner. "Is there an origin to graphic communication?" *Managing Information* 1994, 1:2, 1994, pp.32-34. Reprinted with alterations in his *Information, Knowledge, Text*. Lanham MD: Scarecrow Press, 2001. pp.105-109.
1089. Julian Warner. "Not the exact words: writing, computing, and exactness". Julian Warner, *Information, Knowledge, Text*. Lanham MD: Scarecrow Press, 2001. pp.33-46.
1090. Julian Warner. "Shannon, Weaver and the Minotaur: redundancy in language and information systems". Julian Warner, *Information, Knowledge, Text*. Lanham MD: Scarecrow Press, 2001. pp.17-31.
1091. Julian Warner. "Information and redundancy in the legend of Theseus". **Journal of Documentation** 2003, 59:5, pp.540-557.
1092. Julian Warner. "As sharp as a pen: direct semantic ratification in oral, written, and electronic communication". Julian Warner, *Humanizing information technology*. Lanham, Maryland: Scarecrow Press, 2004. pp.57-67.
1093. Julian Warner. "Materializing communication concepts: linearity and surface in linguistics and information theory". Phil Turner, Susan Turner, Elisabeth Davenport (eds.), *Exploration of Space, Technology, and Spatiality: Interdisciplinary Perspectives*. Hershey PA: Information Science Reference Press. 2008. p. 196-213.
1094. Julian Warner. *Human Information Retrieval*. 1st ed. Cambridge, MA: MIT Press, 2010. viii + 189pp.
1095. Julian Warner. "Creativity for Feist". **Journal of the American Society for Information Science and Technology** 2013, 64:6, pp.1173-1192.

Name Index

Aarsleff, H. 75, 767
Adolf, H. 7
Aitchison, J. 78, 368
Alboul, L. 1066
Allan, K. 307
Allerton, D.J. 373
Alsagoff, L. 855
Altmann, G.T.M. 236
Andrén, M. 600
Anis, J. 784
Ansaldo, U. 975
Araujo, H. 838
Aristotle 256, 332
Arrive, M. 324
Asher, R.E. 187, 244
Ashley, L. 487, 994
Attardo, S. 534
Attlee, J. 309
Augustine 256, 332
Auroux, S. 535, 735
Austin, J. 614, 635
Avalle, D'A.S. 23
Ayer, A.J. 741
Ayres-Bennett, W. 272
Bakhurst, D. 918
Bade, D. 496, 502, 508, 511, 514, 520, 522, 536-539, 592, 687-689, 737, 870, 914, 1009, 1041-1055
Bailey, C.-J. N. 98-100, 139, 360, 984
Baker, G.P. 94
Bakhtin, M. 743

Baldinger, K. 44
Bally, C. 767
Balosa, D. 848
Bansler, J.P. 1056-1057
Barbe, K. 540
Barnett, F.J. 46
Baron, N.S. 472, 541, 785
Barron, C. 941
Bartch, R. 124
Barthes, R. 239
Batalla Rosado, J.J. 828
Beale, P. 96
Beattie, J. 164
Béguin-Verbrugge, A. 786
Bell, R.T. 381
Benjamin, W. 1005
Bennett, W. 401
Benson, J.D. 695
Bentley, M. 489
Berger, L.S. 542, 896
Bernstein, B. 853
Bertelsen, O.W. 1057
Beta, S. 814
Bex, T. 433, 458, 461, 959
Bhaskar, R. 137
Bierce, A. 268
Binnick, R. 688
Bjørn, P. 1055
Blackledge, A. 801
Blakemore, C. 106
Blanche-Benveniste, C. 158
Blavatsky, E. 1004
Bloomfield, L. 752-753

Bocquillon, M. 694
Boissac, P. 242
Bollinger, D. 65
Bolton, K. 691, 871, 932, 940-941, 945, 1010
Bolton, W.F. 91
Bonnafous, S. 762
Borsley, R.D. 394, 417, 543-544
Bouchard, D. 483
Boulanger, J.-C. 683, 1026
Bouquet, Ed. S. 261, 270, 273
Bourdieu, P. 81
Boydens, I. 1052
Braasch, A. 636
Bradford, R. 196
Bratanić, M. 909
Bréal, M. 779
Bright, W. 243
Broadbent, G. 67
Brochu, D. 1064
Brockmeier, J. 269, 787, 806
Brown, K. 294-296
Bruce, N. 941
Bruner, J. 788, 918, 920
Bryant, D. 537
Bryson, B. 96
Bühler, K. 74
Bulajić, V.V. 1080
Bulcaen, C. 443, 456
Bullen, M. 470
Bunt, R. 67
Burchfield, R.W. 76, 268

Burgess, A. 351, 384
Burke, P. 285, 491
Burnley, J.D. 415
Burridge, K. 307
Butler, C.S. 642
Butters, R.R. 1011
Calude, A. 485, 494, 1032
Calvet, L.-J. 111
Camarero, J. 462, 545, 789
Cameron, D. 200, 546, 658, 946-952, 960
Cannon, G. 60
Caron, B. 230
Caron, P. 375
Carr, P. 547-551, 737
Cerquiglini, B. 427
Cezanne, P. 888
Chadwick, J. 383, 426
Chafe, W. 47
Chambers, R. 180
Chan, M. 153-155
Chapman, R. 78
Chapman, S. 442, 447, 552
Charlesworth, J.H. 1008
Chatterjee, R. 403
Chauvet, J.-M. 203
Chomsky, N. 150, 605, 675-677, 680, 753
Chrétien de Troyes 1, 18
Christe, N. 553, 674, 998
Christensen, L.R. 1058-1060
Christensen, W. 696
Christin, A.-M. 826
Chung, K.S. 419

Cicourel, A.V. 369
Cigada, S. 21
Ciolfi, L. 1057
Clark, A. 697
Cloete, M. 790
Clottes, J. 203
Cobley, P. 231, 255-256, 332, 501, 554
Coetzee, C. 742
Cogan, R. 441
Colby, A.M. 26
Collins, C. 908, 973
Collins, J. 206, 208, 211
Comrie, B. 56
Condillac, E. 771, 920
Conger, W. 884
Conley, T. 176
Conrad, C. 897
Contessi, R. 813
Corazza, E. 287
Corbeil, J.-C. 201
Correa, D.A. 791
Cotin, M. 792-793
Cotte, D. 1061-1062
Coulmas, F. 220, 466
Coulter, J. 509, 515, 638
Courtin, J. 203
Covino, S. 253, 811
Cowley, S.J. 555, 698-705
Cowrie, A.P. 87
Cram, D. 731
Cran, W. 103
Creese, A. 801
Crochetiere, A. 683, 1026

Crowley, T. 556, 738-739, 953-955
Cruz-Ferreira, M. 495
Crystal, D. 66, 91, 160, 311, 364, 439-440
Culler, J. 484
Dakhwa, S. 1063
Dalby, A. 232
Dam, J. van 926
Damm, B. 557
Danesi, M. 385
Dardel, R. de 27
Darwin, C. 180
Davallon, J. 794, 1064, 1082
Davenport, E. 1093
David, B. 451
Davies, W.V. 1001
Davis, D.R. 558-559, 849-850, 1012, 1033
Davis, H. 143, 263-264, 450, 523-524, 543, 560-566, 50-581, 596, 610, 616, 648, 657, 925, 956-961, 1013
De Bono, E. 245
De Mauro, T. 192
Deacon, T.W. 215, 667
Debashish, M. 695
DeFrancis, J. 151
Deigh, J. 361
Derrida, J. 191, 206, 208, 211, 240
Desagulier, G. 711
Deschamps, E. Brunel 203
Deuchar, M. 90, 962

Deutscher, G. 292
Diamond, A. 885
Dineen, F. 773
Dirven, R. 936, 943
Dotremont, C. 875
Downing, R.H. 642
Dror, I. 709
Dror, M. 96
Dubois, B.L. 390
Dummett, M. 225, 366
Duncanson, K. 1014
Duncker, D. 567-569, 898-899, 905
Dunn, C.W. 10
Durant, A. 1015
Duranti, A. 812
Eco, U. 102, 237
Edmondson, J.A. 139
Eisenschitz, D. 872
Ellingsen, G. 1056
Embleton, S. 781
Engler, R. 261, 273
Envoy Enterprises 886
Erdal, M. 687
Erneling, C. 732
Esposito, A. 909
Ette, O. 751
Falck, M.J. 600
Farrow, S. 454, 478, 492, 570-572, 706, 933
Feagin, C. 139
Fenn, R.K. 78
Fill, A. 254
Finke, W. 994
Fiorentino, G. 819

Firth, J.R. 758
Fleming, D. 573-574
Fletcher, A. 262
Fodor, J.A. 15
Forel, C.S. 277
Fought, J. 752
Fowler, F. 268
Fowler, H. 268
Frazer, E. 546
Freeman, E. 873
Freud, S. 328
Galarza, J. 808
Galassi, R. 816
Galileo 631, 1040
Galinon-Mélénec, B. 942
Gardiner, A. 768-769
Garron, I. 1065
Gascoigne, L. 488
Gaur, A. 209
Gazdar, G. 353
Genette, G. 194
George, A. 386
Ghimire, G.B. 1063
Ghosh, A. 1066, 1070
Gilderdale, P. 436
Gill, H.S. 162, 241
Glade, F. 473
Goffmann, E. 72
Goldberg, D. 965
Goldstein, L. 422, 707
Gouldner, N. 299-301
Grassi, C. 9
Grasso, M.A. 1057
Gray, P. 260
Grayling, A. 299-301

Greaves, W.S. 695
Green, J. 87, 199
Green, K. 333
Greenbaum, S. 63, 124
Greenfield, S. 106
Gregory, R.L. 507
Greimas, A.J. 131
Grein, M. 929
Gretsch, C. 575
Griffiths, I. 97
Gross, T. 1059, 1078
Grube, G. 290
Guignard, J.-B. 711
Gumperz, J.J. 77, 217
Günther, H. 184, 204
Guy, J. 475
Haadsma, R.A. 11
Haarmann, H. 438
Haas, G. 423
Haas, M. 336, 576, 997-998
Hacker, P.M.S. 94
Hall, P.A.V. 1063
Halliday, M.A.K. 280, 305, 598
Hamilton, C.A. 476
Hannabuss, S. 503
Hansen, A.M. 897, 905
Hardy, D.E. 418
Harnad, S. 709
Harpham, G.G. 740
Harré, R. 95, 137, 172-175, 402, 500, 577, 652, 795, 1034
Harris, J. 165
Harris, Randy 498

Harris, Z. 149
Harrison, A. 449
Harvey, A.J. 1002
Harvey, P. 546
Harvey, S. 887
Harwood, J. 191
Hattori, S. 86
Havn, E.C. 1056-1057
Hawkins, B. 936
Hayhoe, M. 849
Heck, R.G. 225
Heffer, C. 504
Heinimann, S. 12
Heller, L. 96
Hemmingsen, B.H. 626, 900-901
Henton, C. 963
Henze, C. 1067
Heraclitus 264
Herman, D. 477
Hermann, J. 578-579, 690, 888, 902-905
Hernandez de Luna, M. 890
Herreman, A. 1036
Hewson, J. 580
Hillaire, C. 203
Hobson, P. 265
Hoggart, R. 283
Holdcroft, D. 177
Holiday, A. 741-742, 964, 1035
Hollnagel, E. 1045
Holmes, Sherlock 102
Honey, J. 213
Honeybone, P. 737

Hope, T.E. 71
Hopper, P. 581, 743
Hountondji 790
Houssaye, D. 694
Howells, C. 240
Hoyois, L. 906
Hu, G. 855
Huddart, D. 996
Hudson, K. 87
Hughes, R. 429
Hüllen, W. 582, 744
Humboldt, W. von 256, 332, 761
Humez, A. 96
Humphrey, C. 831, 834, 837
Hunte, H.R. 218
Hurford, J.R. 312
Huspek, M. 973
Hussel, E. 328
Hutton, C.M. 310, 583-592, 794 633, 691, 744-751, 851-852, 871, 873, 932, 934-941, 945, 965-969, 1003-1004, 1009-1011, 1014-1025, 1029
Inkpen, K. 1059, 1078
Innis, R.E. 74
Inoue, K. 86
Ionita, M. 465
Irigaray, L. 320
Irigoin, J. 134
Jackendoff, R. 259
Jacko, J. 1063
Jackson, J.R. de J. 147
Jacobsen, N.D. 506

Jakobson, R. 216, 1055
Jamison, C.P. 463
Janich, P. 1044
Jansen, T. 267
Janson, T. 288
Jaspers, J. 457
Jeanneret, Y. 942, 1064, 1068, 1081-1083
Jencks, C. 67
Johnson, D. 732
Johnson, M. 145
Johnson-Laird, P.N. 59
Jones, K.P. 1085
Jones, P.E. 593, 631, 853, 907-908, 970-973, 1066, 1069-1070, 1073-1074
Jones, W. 168
Jordan, M.P. 135
Joseph, J.E. 144, 216, 248, 378, 460, 527, 556, 594-597, 649, 752-756, 781, 804, 864-865, 949, 974, 1004, 1026
Junod, K. 997
Jutant, C. 1071
Kant, I. 889
Karas, H. 480
Katz, J.J. 15
Kaye, A.S. 379, 437, 455, 481
Keller, E. 909
Keller, R. 233
Kerler, D.-B. 745
Kern, R. 855
Kibbee, D.A. 589

Kilpert, D. 598
King, B.J. 725, 729
Kirk, R. 105
Klinkenberg, J.-M. 796
Knight, N. 1000
Knowles, E. 252
Koerner, K. 772
Kogge, W. 290
Komatsu, E. 171
Korżyk, K. 909
Kovacs, S. 1065
Krämer, S. 290, 797
Kravchenko, A.V. 599-601, 705, 708-715, 717
Kroskrity, P.V. 974
Krzyzek, P. 694
Kunøe, M. 899
Küster, M.W. 486
Kuzar, R. 602
Lamarque, P. 222, 399, 408
Langer, N. 1001
Lapacherie, G. 223-224
Lapaire, J-R 711
Lapierrre, L. 218
Läpple, D. 969
Lass, R. 757
Lavid, J. 642
Lavis, G. 51
Lear, J. 362
Leather, J.H. 926
Lee, C. 996
Lee, D. 603
Leech, G. 63
Legrand, J. 692
Lehmann, W.P. 412

Leith, D. 80
Lemarechal, A. 448
Le Marec, J. 1064, 1081
Lemke, J.L. 428
Levin, S. 387, 391
Levinson, S.C. 217
Levy, G. 1005-1007
Liang, R. 604
Lier, L. van 861
Linell, P. 716-717, 798
Linn, A. 731
Linn, M.D. 411
Lintern, G. 910
Locke, F.W. 6
Locke, J. 767, 770, 773
Lopes, D. 219
Love, N. 39, 45, 50, 53, 55, 71, 86, 93, 95, 112, 140-141, 205, 297-298, 400, 517-518, 528, 533, 541, 544, 548, 574, 577, 595, 605-618, 640, 683, 693, 702, 718, 740, 749, 754-760, 774-777, 805, 835, 889, 919, 975, 980, 1035
Lucie-Smith, E. 316
Ludwig, O. 184, 204
Lund, S. 539, 619
Lundmark, C. 600
Lussu, G. 799-800
Lyons, J. 70, 78, 410
MacCabe, C. 260
MacGregor, G. 646
Mackin, R. 87
MacNamara, J. 89

MacNeil, R. 103
Mahboob, A. 1000
Maillat, D. 997
Maine, H. 873
Makoni, S.B. 801, 976-979
Malinowski, B. 766, 944
Malmberg, B. 780
Manandhar, P. 1063
Mancini, M. 829, 843
Manetti, G. 241, 783
Martinet, A. 420
Marx, K. 972
Masson, P. 968
Maturana, H. 713
Maxwell, E.J.J. 120
Maxwell, E.R. 345
Mayblin, B. 206, 208, 211
Mazzeo, M. 813
McCaig, I.R. 87
McCrum, R. 103
McCullagh, C. Behan 490
McDonough, R. 444
McGilfray, J.A. 358
McHale, B. 371, 392, 395
Mckay, S.L. 855
McWhorter, J.H. 267
Meek, M. 92
Meillet, A. 980
Meisenburg, T. 425
Melby, A. 866
Menary, R. 802
Menz, A. 687
Merrell, F. 190
Messling, M. 751, 969
Meyer, M. 1038, 1048

Meyer-Lübke, W. 34
Meynard, C. 694
Michaels, L. 136
Michaux, H. 875
Mignolo, W.D. 838
Millar, R.M. 980
Miller, G.A. 59
Miller, J. 92
Minel, J.-L 1065
Mitchell, W.J.T. 185
Mitford, M. 268
Moignet, G. 25
Mollerup, P. 209
Monet, C. 888
Mønsted, T. 1056-1057
Moore, G.E. 115, 119
Moore, T. 413
Morandina, B. 816
Moreno Cabrera, J.C. 620-621, 803, 981-983
Morris, M. 864, 867
Mufwene, S. 622
Mühlhäusler, P. 139, 254, 482, 623, 719-720, 761, 804, 943, 984-988
Mühlschlegel, U. 968
Müller, M. 181
Munz, V. 335
Murray, A. 179
Murray, J. 115, 119
Myers, D. 720
Nagarjuna 264
Nair, R.B. 854
Nanayakara, T. 1073-1074
Nash, J. 989

Nelson, M.E. 855
Nerlich, B. 624
Nevskaya, I. 687
Newmeyer, F.J. 111, 544, 623
Niederehe, H.-J. 772, 781
Nielsen, C.B. 888, 911-916
Noel-Cadet, N. 1064, 1072
Noren, S.J. 346
Nowak, E. 731
Nuchelmans, J. 11
Nunan, D. 941
Nuttall, S. 742
Ogden, C.K. 778
O'Grady, P. 405
O'Hara, K. 429
O'Hara, R.C. 396
Olson, D.R. 212, 269, 329, 471, 787-788, 805-807
Oore, I. 218
Orman, J. 856, 989-992
Orwell, G. 148
Östman, J-O. 313-314
O'Sullivan, M. 996
Ouellon, C. 683, 1026
Owen, C. 857
Owen, D.D.R. 49
Pablé, A. 522, 539, 591-593, 625-633, 856, 917, 993-998, 1037, 1040
Page, A. 445
Palma, A. 721
Panini 783
Papadopoulos, G.A. 1057
Parker, S. 849

Partridge, E. 66, 87, 96
Pateman, T. 609, 889
Pau-Fuk, P. 1010
Paveau, A.-M.-A. 762
Pedrazzini, A.M. 874
Peirce, C. 667
Pelard, E. 875
Peletier du Mans, J. 29
Pelkey, J.R. 869
Pelletier, J. 807
Penders, J. 1066, 1070, 1073-1074
Peng X. 634
Pennycook, A. 979, 999-1000
Percival, W.K. 370
Perri, A. 229, 275, 800, 808-830
Perrin, O. 831-834, 837
Peter, L. 852
Pettersson, J.S. 435, 835
Pfeffer, W. 764
Philip, L. 694
Pickens, R.T. 764
Pier, J. 430
Pierson, S. 474
Pim, J.E. 831, 834, 836-837
Pine, L.G. 87
Pinker, S. 188
Plato 790
Plöckinger, O. 765
Polzenhagen, F. 852
Pontecorvo, C. 158
Porter, R. 152
Porter, S.E. 1008

Porteau, P. 30
Porter, L.C. 29
Posner, R. 32, 221
Poulle, E. 134
Povlsen, C. 636
Pratt, M.L. 359
Priestley, J. 167
Prilutski, N. 745
Proffitt, M. 213
Pryor, S. 858, 891-893
Puhl, K. 335
Pütz, M. 761, 943
Pyle, A. 299-301
Quine, W. 681
Quirk, R. 348
Ragagnin, E. 689
Rai, A. 148
Rajagopalan, K. 635
Rampton, M.B.H. 546
Ranasinghe, A. 1073
Rapko, J. 516
Raskin, V. 347
Rathje, M. 898
Raynaud, M.-L. 424
Read, H. 1066, 1070
Renandya, W.A. 855
Reuland, E.J. 121
Revelli, C. 1051
Reynolds, V. 95
Rhea, B. 1008
Rheinfelder, H. 38
Ricento, T. 999
Richardson, K. 546
Ricks, C. 136
Ritzau, U. 856

Robins, R.H. 416
Robinson, D. 868
Robinson, I. 404
Roger, L. 636
Rorty, R. 632
Rosenstock-Huessy, E. 537-538
Ross, D. 722
Rothschild, V. 260
Rotman, B. 323
Rousseau, J.J. 789
Royle, N. 191
Russell, B. 333, 338
Russo, T. 813
Ruz Barrio, M.A. 828
Ryan, D. 512
Saito S. 214
Salkie, R. 510
Salomon, F. 838
Salus, P.H. 414
Sampson, G. 363, 469
Sampson, R. 272
Samuels, D.W. 453
Sanders, C. 377, 479
Sandikcioglu, E. 936
Sanitt, N. 1038-1039
Sassi, M. 814
Sassoon, R. 209
Saussure, F. 84, 107, 116, 159, 171, 175, 177, 192, 210, 214, 216, 218, 247-249, 256, 261, 270, 273, 277-279, 302, 314, 324, 330, 332, 337, 375-378, 395-407, 411-416, 419-421, 475-480,

483-484, 624, 739, 753, 781, 865
Saussure, L. de 302
Savage-Rumbaugh, S. 238, 695, 723-724, 726
Schalkwyk, D. 306
Schiavino, F. 840
Schieffelin, B.B. 974
Schleifer, R. 131
Schmandt-Besserat, D. 388
Schmidt, K.H. 434, 452
Schmidt, Kj. 1056-1057, 1075-1078
Schmoll, L. 1079
Schneider, J.G. 304, 318
Schopenhauer, A. 895
Scrivano, F. 817, 839-840
Seaman, B. 1080
Searle, J. 615, 630, 635
Sebeok, T.A. 102
Seuren, P.A.M. 226
Shanker, S.G. 238, 637, 723-726, 731-732, 918, 925
Shannon, C. 1090
Sharrock, W. 509, 515, 638
Shaumyan, S. 123
Shelvador, C. 432
Sherwin, R.K. 1024
Shipley, J. 96
Siiner, M. 639, 888
Simpson, J.M.Y. 187, 380
Singh, H. 783
Sinsheimer, A. 1027
Sirat, C. 134, 841

Skovgaard-Petersen, K. 897, 905
Slater, C. 640
Smith, A. 163
Smith, N. 353
Smith, N.V. 350
Souchier, E. 842, 876, 1064-1065, 1081
Spurrett, D. 499, 529, 631, 727, 1040
Stafford, A. 239
Stafford, B.M. 152
Steiner, G. 251
Stewart, D. 180
Stockwell, P. 641
Stoevsky, A. 642
Stopyra, J. 643
Stork, F.C. 356
Strang, B. 354
Strawson, P.F. 680
Street, R.L. 365
Sturrock, J. 376, 464
Sugeta, S. 192
Süselbeck, K. 968
Sutton, J. 728
Svartvik, J. 63
Sweet, H. 180
Swift, J. 739
Szymura, J. 766
Svendsen, J.H. 1057
Svenstrup, L. 898
Taglialatela, J. 695
Takahara, P.O. 374
Takizawa N. 214
Tallerman, M. 292

Tardy, C. 1082-1083
Taschek, W. 398
Taylor, J.R. 919
Taylor, T.J. 129, 143-144, 146, 210, 214, 238, 263-264, 523-524, 527, 530, 534, 543, 556, 560, 566, 580-582, 586, 596-597, 610, 616, 644-659, 723-724, 726, 729-732, 753-755, 767-774, 804, 877-879, 918, 920-925, 949
Temmar, M. 762
Ter Meulen, A.G.B. 121
Teubert, W. 660-661
Thapa, I. 1063
Thibault, P.J. 247
Thomas, M. 216
Thorpe, L. 8
Tietze, A. 894
Tilander, G. 5
Timini, I. 1065
Tobin, Y. 161, 421
Tolar, M. 1078
Tooke, J.H. 166
Toolan, M. 217, 325, 393, 459, 505, 531, 637, 641, 662-666, 684, 775, 850-851, 854, 857-860, 862, 879-882, 1028-1029
Torrance, N. 212, 329
Toussaint, M. 104
Trabant, J. 969
Trench, R.C. 182
Trudgill, P. 61
Tsohatzidis, S.L. 142

Turchetta, B. 829, 843
Turner, P. 1093
Turner, S. 1003
Tuttle, J. 1055
Ullmann, S. 71
Unger, J.M. 431, 446
Urton, G. 838
Urwin, K. 13
Väänänen, V. 42
Vargas Mendoza, J.E. 927
Verschueren, J. 313-314
Verspoor, M. 761
Vierne, B. 211
Vihla, M. 407
Villiers, T. 667
Villon, François 20
Vygotsky, L. 907, 931
Wagner, A. 1024
Wagner, I. 1076-1078
Waldron, T.P. 352
Wales, K. 397
Walicek, D.E. 493
Walrod, M. 776, 869, 928-929
Wan, M. 1022
Wang, J. 335
Wang, M. 269, 787-788, 807
Warner, J. 844, 1084-1095
Washabaugh, W. 406
Waterhouse, K. 68
Watt, W.C. 389, 468
Watts, R. 959
Wawrzyńak, J. 497, 668-669

Weaver, W. 1090
Weber, J.-J. 879
Webster, J. 280, 305
Weigand, E. 670-673, 777, 862, 928-929
Weightman, J. 276, 355, 382
Weiner, E.S.C. 87
Wells, J.C. 73
Wenger, J. 553, 674
Werry, C. 675-677, 733
Wheeler, M. 734
Whitney, W.D. 183
Whorf, B.L. 761
Widell, P. 578-579, 899
Wiegand, H.E. 797
Wilding, M.J. 349
Wilkerson, D. 883
Wilkerson, K.T. 883
Willensky, J. 186
Williams, S.W. 748, 1003
Willson, P. 235
Wiseman, N. 180
Witczak-Plisiecka, I. 1030-10031
Wittgenstein, L. 116, 175, 335, 398-407, 559, 577, 644
Worsøe, L.B. 930

Wolf, G. 93, 112, 132, 135, 139-140, 156-157, 162, 205, 228, 518, 526, 532-533, 541, 544, 548, 561, 571, 574, 577, 583, 585, 595, 603, 607, 610, 613, 622, 645-646, 650, 659, 664, 666, 678-683, 694, 739, 764, 778-783, 795, 805, 835, 845, 849, 867, 880, 889, 895, 919, 944, 947, 950, 958, 963, 985, 1016, 1035
Wolf, H.-G. 852
Woods, D.D. 1045
Woolard, K.A. 974
Yatsenko, S.A. 831, 834, 837
Yolton, J.W. 152
Žegarac, V. 513
Zgusta, L. 409, 684
Zhang R. 863, 931
Zhang T.S. 685
Zhou F. 686
Ziltener, W. 4
Zinna, A. 846-847
Zlatev, J. 600
Zorella, C. 816

www.ingramcontent.com/pod-product-compliance
Lightning Source LLC
Chambersburg PA
CBHW072047290426
44110CB00014B/1586